THE EQUITY ADVANTAGE

YOUR GOLDEN TICKET TO BUILDING A THRIVING PROPERTY PORTFOLIO

Jason Hare

Table of Contents

ACKNOWLEDGEMENTS

To Kate, for giving me the reasons to strive for more.

To Sam Panetta and Jackson Millan, your teachings on business success and frank advice on presenting a best seller have made all the difference.

Thanks Nick, for your time and advice with the editing process; it has been invaluable.

To Mum, you have the greatest work ethic I have ever seen. I have created this so that others never have to work as hard as you.

ABOUT THE AUTHOR

From my own experience building a multi-million-dollar property portfolio and helping hundreds of other investors do the same, I have discovered the key elements required to build wealth through property.

I will guide you on how and when to use those same principles. All while staying within your own personal risk tolerance. I will show you how to use your most valuable asset to its fullest and achieve your goals faster than you ever thought possible.

Through my 15 years of property investing and helping others build huge property portfolios as a finance consultant, I have a tried and tested method that will fit any investment strategy.

I will teach you how to use your Equity Advantage.

FOREWORD

From a young age, I knew that working till the age of 65 was not for me. I didn't see the point in working almost half my life to then retire on a tiny income and hope that I am still healthy enough to enjoy my remaining years left on this earth.

While I worked in the defence industry for much of my earlier years, on the side, I was looking for that get-rich-quick scheme that would make me millions. Well, that obviously didn't happen, and those schemes most certainly did not work out as they were advertised.

But the desire to be free to do whatever I wished never left me. I refused to accept that a 9-5, 5 days a week with a few weeks off over Christmas was my future.

I think the desire to be free of the constraints of "work" comes from a very young age.

My mother is literally the hardest working person I have ever seen. At 65 she still works 7 days a week. I wish I could say that its by choice. Watching her struggle and work through adversity is truly inspirational but also heartbreaking.

When I was 26, I was lucky enough to purchase my first house. I never realised at the time, but that property would be the first step to building a multi-million-dollar portfolio. I could never have conceived that I could use that one property to propel myself to more and more properties until I could retire decades earlier than expected!!

Now just to be clear- I have not retired yet. Although I have set a goal date, so the challenge is on.

Over the last 15 years, I have changed strategies 3-4 times. Been delayed years on certain projects and sold properties undervalued and (prior to my property education) even lost $40,000 on one property purchase/sale. And still, I have managed to improve my financial situation drastically by using property as my vehicle.

You see, even if you lose money on one property, that "loss" can be carried forward and used in later years when you make a big capital gain. Understanding the way our Australian property rules operate can save you tens of thousands of dollars. So, if you stay in the game long enough, you can always make your money back.

Over that time, I have bought and sold many properties, and as of the writing of this book, my wife and I have a portfolio of close to $3,600,000. That's not to brag. That's just a piece of evidence that I walk the walk, not just talk the talk.

What I'm going to teach you is how to go from one to six or even ten properties while making as few mistakes as possible. And certainly not the same mistakes I made.

This book is designed as a step-by-step guide on how to use your properties' Equity correctly to supercharge the speed of building your portfolio. It also includes tips on how to budget, save, choose a strategy, obtain finance, research a location, choose a property, make an offer, and settle the deal to then rinse and repeat so that you can buy as many properties as your goal requires. With this book and me as your guide im going to show you your hidden superpower.

If you have the intention to hit huge goals and use property to maximise your wealth, then don't just read this book. Get in contact with my team and we can kick start your investment journey.

The best property investors in Australia all have an advantage that they use to win auctions, to grow huge portfolios, build massive developments and to create generational wealth.

The Equity Advantage.

And I'm going to teach it to you.

1

THE BENEFITS OF A PROPERTY PORTFOLIO

When it comes to investing, there are a lot of baskets to choose from: real estate, shares, bonds, gold, and options, just to name a few.

Every one of the assets listed above takes a certain level of understanding and knowledge before you can successfully create wealth with them.

The great thing about property as an investment is that everyone has had some experience with property.

Whether you own or rent, you are aware and understand, on a basic level, the need and use for a home. Having a basic knowledge of an asset before using it as an investment tool is vital.

Another incredible reason why real estate is used by more Australians as an investment tool than any other asset class (not including Super) is that we have some very beneficial government legislation that assist all homeowners. Let me list a few:

1. Owner Occupiers (OOCC) pay no Capital Gains Tax (CGT) on the sale of their own property if they have owned it for longer than 12 months. Many older Australians are making a killing using this benefit due to the fact their properties have tripled or quadrupled in value. When it comes time to downsize, they simply sell and keep 100% of the profits.

2. Depreciation: This is the ability to claim a tax deduction on the decreasing value of your investment property and the items within.

3. Negative gearing: This is where you claim the interest that you have paid on an investment loan over a financial year. For example, if you own an investment property, and you have paid $10,000 in interest for a year, and you earned $100,000 from your job or business that you paid tax on, then you can have $10,000 deducted from your income, meaning you only earned $90,000. For the extra $10,000 that you paid tax on, you will receive a refund back from the ATO.

4. 50% capital gains tax exemption: This allows you to only pay tax on 50% of the profits you made from an investment if you owned it for longer than 12 months.

5. Six-year rule: This rule means that if you own and live in a property and then turn it into an investment property (then do not nominate another primary place of residence) for six years after you no longer live in that property, you will not

have to pay CGT on any profits earned from the sale of that property.

6. EQUITY: In Australia, unlike many other countries in the world. We are allowed to release equity to use for other purposes.

These are just a few of the ways that real estate in Australia is being promoted and 'protected' by the government. Any person can take advantage of these 'benefits,' even you.

What's your Why?

It's important to understand all your options before you actually invest your money and start to build your portfolio.

One of the main reasons that people say they want to build a property portfolio is to retire early.

A. Retirement:

Building a retirement-grade property portfolio does not happen overnight. It's not a get-rich-quick scheme, no matter what you read in the media. It's a decade or more, long journey of budgeting, goal setting, due diligence, finance approvals, renovations, and in some cases, poor tenants.

It's hard. Don't let anyone tell you any different. So, prepare yourself or protect yourself with knowledge so you don't make the same mistakes as many other investors (including myself) have made.

B. With a property portfolio comes the spoils:

The rewards of owning a well-structured and intelligently purchased portfolio can be incredible. Imagine being retired at 30, 40, or 50, depending on when you start, with enough passive income every week to never have to worry about an electricity bill and to have enough cash in your account to take an impromptu trip overseas a couple of times a year.

C. Leaving your properties to your kids:

I would hazard a guess and say most parents want the best for their children. Being able to gift them or help with a house deposit is a great way to give them a leg up. Property ownership in 10 – 15 years may be a lot harder than it currently is.

As I will discuss later, having that first property under your belt to use as leverage is a big help; it's almost unfair. I'm ok with giving my kids as much of an advantage in life as I can give them.

D. Choice:

Choice is the number one benefit of owning a well-structured multi-million-dollar portfolio. You can choose to work or not, get up when the alarm goes off or not, or choose to play with your kids all day, play golf when you want, or take your wife on a lunch date. You choose!

A well-structured property portfolio of 4-6 properties will provide you with enough passive income to retire and live a pretty kick-ass life.

In the following chapters, I'm going to show you how.

If you know your why then don't put off starting on your goals one more day. Its time to act.

Investment Tip #1- Australia has the world's most advantageous taxation benefits for property owners. Make use of them while they are still around because one day, they will be gone.

2

COMMONLY USED TERMS IN REAL ESTATE AND FINANCE AND WHAT THEY MEAN

LVR: Loan to Value Ratio: The ratio of your loan to your property's value. Calculated as Loan Remaining divided by Property Value X 100 = **LVR**

Loan Remaining $\div$ Property Value X 100 = **LVR**

For example: $500,000 (loan remaining) divided by $800,000 (value of property) X 100 = **62.5% LVR**

LMI: Lenders Mortgage Insurance: Insurance the bank requires you to pay for loans over 80% LVR. This insurance protects the **bank** if you default, **not you.**

Equity: The difference between your property's value and what you still owe.

Equity = *Property Value - Remaining Loan*

Eg: $800,000 - $500,000 = $300,000.

Useable Equity: The amount the bank will allow you to **use** of the above amount.

Property Value X 0.8 – Remaining Loan = **Useable Equity at 80% LVR**

Learn this formula. It is the foundation of this book.

Cash Flow: The excess cash you have at the end of the month after all your expenses OR an investment strategy where you try to achieve a cash flow every month from your portfolio, generally at the expense of capital growth.

Capital growth: The growth of your property's value from the day you purchased it OR an investment strategy where you seek your properties to increase in value (usually at the expense of cash flow).

Deductible Interest: Interest charged on investment loans is tax deductible.

Depreciation: The decrease in an asset's value: In property, it is classed as the plant and equipment and the fixtures and fittings. As these decrease in value over time, you can claim these as a deduction to your taxable income. An example of this would be a kitchen stove if it was purchased brand new, and its value decreased each year. That decrease in value can be deducted from your taxable income.

Offset account: An account used to store savings to decrease the interest payable on a loan. Example: If your home loan is $500,000 and you have $100,000 in an offset account linked to that loan, then you will only pay interest on $400,000. Your repayments will stay the same; however, the extra you save on interest goes to paying down your principal portion of the loan, paying it off faster, and taking years off your loan.

Redraw account: Similar to an offset, although your extra funds are deposited into your actual loan account and reduce the interest paid.

The downside of a redraw is that you can be charged a fee to access your funds, and there may be limits restricting the amount you can remove or deposit. The bank can also 'claim' those funds and reduce your loan limit without consent which happened to a few thousand ME bank customers a few years ago. The public outcry was large and loud.

IO: IO is Interest Only which is a repayment type, meaning you only pay the interest accrued and not the principal. After 5 years (the normal IO term), you will not have paid any off your original loan (the principal), and your repayments will convert to P+I for the remaining 25 years of your loan. These repayments will be higher due to the shorter period in which to pay down your loan.

P+I: Principal and Interest: A repayment method where you will pay the interest and a portion of the principal (loan) down each month.

Variable and Fixed: Variable is the type of interest rate structure you have chosen. A variable rate will go up and down depending on the bank's whim and that of the RBA's (Reserve Bank of Australia) current cash rate.

A fixed rate is a fixed interest rate that will not change for the chosen period. Usually 1 – 5 years. Normally, fixed rates are more expensive than variable, though they give customers confidence in their repayments, as it stays the same over a known period.

It allows them to plan and budget for the future, though, throughout history, variable rates have traditionally saved customers more than fixed rates.

Stamp Duty/Transfer Tax: It is a state tax imposed when the title of a property is exchanged.

Cross Collateralization: When two properties are considered one security by the lender-see Chapter 13 for my thoughts on this.

Security: The property that the loan is 'secured' against.

COS: Contract of Sale: The contract for a property or parcel of land.

COC: Certificate of Currency: Insurance policy for your property.

Splits: When you have one loan amount split into separate smaller loans. E.g., a $300,000 equity loan made up of 3 x $100,000 splits.

BC – Borrowing Capacity: It is the size of loan a lender will allow you to borrow for a particular income, debt, and specific scenario.

Now that we have a grasp on the weird terms and acronyms used in the industry, let's jump straight in and learn how Equity really is Nitrous Oxide for any fast-track property investor.

Investment Tip #2 – With a lower LVR, you can negotiate a better interest rate.

3

EQUITY: THE GOLDEN TICKET

Let's jump right in; I know you are keen to get into the nuts and bolts.

Equity!

We hear it spoken about by everybody. The media, your mates around the BBQ, your wife's best friend, your accountant and every investment educator worth their salt and some that aren't. They throw the term 'equity' around as if it's this tangible thing that you can use to get rich just by saying the word.

But what is Equity?

Equity in its simplest form, when it relates to property, is the difference between what your property is valued and how much you still owe against the property.

If your property is valued at $1,000,000, and you still owe $500,000, then you have $500,000 in equity, right?

Simple.

Well, not so fast! There is a little more to it than that.

That full $500,000 of equity cannot all be used to buy another property, for example. It's also not $500,000 in cash that the bank will just give you.

Due to the bank's aversion to risk, they like to keep a safe buffer between what your property is worth and what they will allow you to borrow against it.

In the same way, as you cannot borrow 100% of a property; (you require a deposit) with equity, the bank requires they keep 20% of your property's value as a safeguard against market fluctuations and the possibility that you don't repay your loan, and they need to sell it to recover costs.

So, using the above figures of a $1,000,000 property, with a $500,000 loan, the bank would calculate 80% of $1,000,000, so $800,000, and then subtract what you still owe, in this case, $500,000. Leaving you with $300,000 in usable equity. Remember that term. Useable equity.

Simplified it's:

$1,000,000 (Value) X 0.8 = 80% of your property's value or $800,000.

$800,000 – (minus) $500,000 (what you still owe) = $300,000 in Usable Equity

Now, if you are ok with a higher level of risk, then the bank will allow you to borrow up to 90% of the value of your property (It's the same calculation but with .9 instead of .8) though they will charge you 'Lenders Mortgage Insurance' (LMI).

This is insurance that you pay (usually, the bank adds the cost of LMI to your loan), and it protects the *bank* if you default. It's not there to protect you.

That sounds like a bad deal, right? Well, maybe. We'll discuss this more later.

As a rule, I try to stay at 80% LVR or below. If you are in a real hurry to build your portfolio and have zero worries about the higher risk involved, then a 90% LVR may be an acceptable option. But for me, with a family and kids to consider, 80% LVR is where I'm comfortable.

So, here we are, with $300,000 of usable equity. But how does that equity become something I can use? Does the bank just give me $300k?

So NOW we enter the crux of the Equity Advantage:

The bank allows you to borrow that equity/cash money from them. So, in this case, you will take out a loan of $300,000, and then, they will give you $300,000 in cash. Now, your equity is real. It now exists. It is now tangible.

As an investor, what is the best way to borrow that equity? Should we take it in one lump sum? Should we release it as a principal and interest loan or an interest-only loan?

Should it be added to your Owner Occupier home loan?

And how do you use this new cash that the bank has just lent you to buy a new property?

Do we buy a $300,000 property outright?

The answer is very simple, though thousands of investors get it wrong every year and it costs them dearly. Getting this right will ensure you can continue to invest and will protect you as an investor. Low risk is where I prefer to operate from when investing.

It's as simple as A, B & C.

In fact, that's what I call it - A, B & C.

Let's go through a scenario of a Self-Employed individual wanting to use the ABC Equity Advantage.

Step A is to Refinance your existing home.

Step B is to Release your equity as a separate loan with its own offset account.

Step C is to get pre-approval for the amount you wish to use to purchase an investment property.

Now, let's unpack the A, B & C in a little more detail.

Self-Employed example of using the A, B & C Equity Advantage:

Step A: You are about to release $300,000 in equity from your 'Own Home,' which you will use as deposits to help buy two more properties. In this scenario, the applicant wants to purchase two properties, so it's smarter to release enough equity for the second property at the same time as the first.

You will refinance your existing home with a lender that will lend to self-employed applicants with specific business requirements (Ensuring the bank's policy matches your income requirements is essential).

You will ensure that the lender has a 'cash out' policy (cash out is Equity in the finance industry) that will allow you to release $300,000 for investment purposes.

Some lenders have limitations on how much cash out (equity) they will allow you to release.

Step B: The cash out will be released as its own 5-year Variable Interest Only loan with an offset.

We do this so that once your equity is released, you can place the $300,000 in the offset account, and as your loan is IO, you won't make any repayments.

WHAT, NO REPAYMENTS AT ALL?

None at all, while those two amounts are balanced. If you spend $1 of your $300,000, you begin to pay interest and make repayments on $1.

If your loans are not structured like this, then you need to have it fixed as soon as possible. Call our team at Open Plan Finance and we will correct any mistakes the banks or previous brokers have made.

You need to have your properties structured correctly to form the foundation of your portfolio. Or it could cost you years, hundreds of thousands of dollars and many potential future investment opportunities if you don't.

No Payment Interest Only Loan Structure

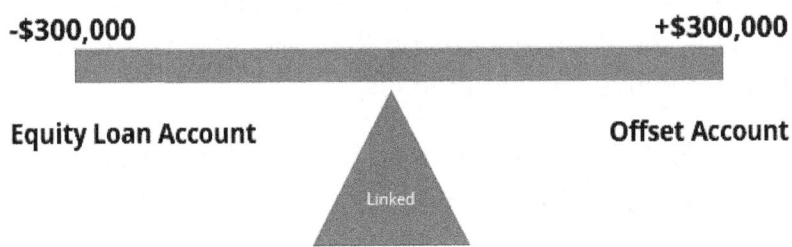

-$300,000   **+$300,000**

Equity Loan Account   **Offset Account**

Linked

You could effectively have $300,000 in an account while you look for the 'right' property for 5 years and never have to pay a cent in repayments.

And if you don't want to keep the 'cash out' after the 5 years IO loan limit, then you can simply ask the bank to close out your account. No harm, no foul. This is truly one of the best benefits of equity when it is set up correctly.

Step C: Pre-approval for your purchase loan amount. Easy.

And the good news is that A, B & C can all be done at the same time. So, you only have to gather one lot of documents. You get three applications for the effort of one.

But what do we use the equity for?

The equity is to be used for your deposits!

Depending on the price of the properties you are looking to buy, your equity should be rationed and stretched as far as possible.

So, don't go putting down a $300,000 deposit on a million-dollar property.

You could, but that's all your equity gone in one go.

If your risk profile and buying rules have indicated that you want to buy property in the $650,000 price range, then you would split your equity up into as many deposits as possible and as many purchases as your borrowing capacity will allow.

That's why you are much better off using a broker that can calculate your borrowing capacity for purchases 1, 2 and 3. It's vital- you need to know you will have the best chance of being approved for all your intended purchases when you release your equity.

There is no point in releasing $300,000 in equity if all you can afford is one investment property.

In the above scenario, I would try to squeeze three $650,000 properties out of that amount of equity.

The breakdown is as follows. A 12% deposit for a $650,000 property is $78,000.

Why a 12% deposit, you ask?

Because it's the minimum amount you need as an investor to use 99% of all banks and lenders.

The majority of the banks and non-banks in Australia have a 90% LVR threshold for all investment purchases. That's their policy, and you can't get around it. Yes, there are some lenders that will go to 95%, but the LMI fees skyrocket once your LVR hits 90% and over.

So a 12% deposit is the sweet spot of a manageable LMI fee and maximising your deposit.

A 12% deposit is because we are above the 80% LVR range that banks like, which means they will slug you with Lenders Mortgage Insurance. As mentioned before, the bank will add your LMI fee to your loan amount. So, let's look at the figures for this scenario.

$650,000 X 0.12 = $78,000 or 12% deposit, which leaves a loan amount of $572,000 or 88% loan

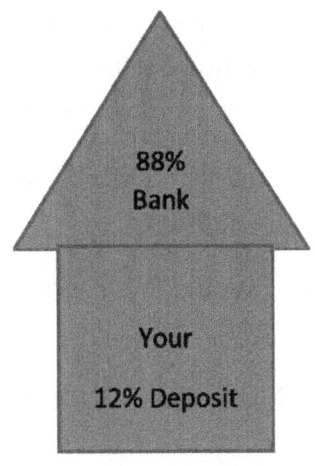

This is 88% of the value of the $650,000 property. When the bank adds LMI onto your loan, as a rough guide, it will be slightly less than 2% of the property's value.

So, when LMI is added to your loan at settlement, your LVR will sit just under the 90% threshold and therefore, still within bank policy. So, as an investor, start thinking of 12% deposits as the norm. Take 10% deposits out of your mindset.

So, $78,000 for a 12% deposit and then add $25,000 for stamp duty (for an existing property). Total of $103,000.

Same again for purchase two, and then for purchase three, you will be a little bit short, so you reduce your purchase limit for the third property. This way, you have purchased three properties very close to your target range and maximised your equity release of $300,000 by purchasing three properties from just one equity release.

In one year, you can go from owning one property to owning four. All with the help of using the Equity Advantage and it's as simple as A, B, &C.

Your equity can also be used for any renovations that your property may need, any solicitor costs, buyers' agents' fees and anything that is investment related.

It's not advisable to use equity released for investment use for personal purposes unless you have specifically split your equity for that purpose. It makes tax time and calculating your deductions tricky if you do.

How much should my pre-approval be?

If your maximum Borrowing Capacity (BC) is a $500,000 loan, then that's what we apply for. It's much easier to change your loan to a lower amount than to increase it above what was pre-approved.

So, after a year of purchasing, you now have 4 properties and zero equity left. What do you do now?

Well, 4 properties could be all you require if they are good investment stock. If you have planned that you need 5 or 6 properties in your portfolio to retire or whatever your goal may be. Then you will need to wait for the market to create more equity through organic growth.

Or you can create capital growth yourself by improving a property so that it achieves a higher valuation than when you bought it. The good thing is you have four properties to release equity from, so obtaining your last one or two deposits from equity should not be that hard.

The A, B, & C is the rinse and repeat process you can use for every purchase moving forward, so you don't have to use your own hard-earned cash that you have already paid tax on.

Another reason why equity is your golden ticket and gives you such an advantage is that it is Tax-Free! You take it out, use it and don't pay any tax on it. You pay a small amount in interest, but on the whole, it's tax-free. This is why 'I LOVE EQUITY.'

Did you also notice that we are actually borrowing 100% of the property's value? You can't borrow 100% as a traditional buyer, but having an existing property to release equity from, means you have now structured your way around that bank rule!!

How to keep all your accounts in order!

Having multiple loan accounts and offset accounts can get confusing. See the following for how to keep track of all your accounts in an easy and simple manner.

Examples of how to structure and label your loan accounts for property investors.

1. Example of how your loans and offsets should be structured and labelled if you have your own home and one investment property.

Name of account	Loan Balance		Name of Offset	Benefit
Owner Occupier Homeloan	-$500,000 usually at P+I variable	Linked	O-OccOffset- All spare income should be placed here. Even if it's just for 1-2 days. Including salary	Any funds in this offset will reduce the interest you pay on your O-Occ home loan
Equity Release Loan to be used for investment purposes	-$120,000 usually IO variable	Linked	EquityRelease Offset +$120,000	While these two amounts are equal no repayments will be required. When funds are used for investment purposes, such as your deposit then this interest becomes tax deductible also
Investment Property-A Loan	-$500,000 can be P+I or IO (variable or fixed)		No offset is required as this is fully tax deductible	

2. Example of how your loans and offsets should be structured and labelled if you have an own home and two investment properties having released equity in two splits of $100,000 to be used for each deposit.

Name of Account	Loan Balance		Name of Offset	Benefit
Owner Occupier Homeloan	-$500,000 usually at P+I variable	Linked	O-OccOffset- All spare income should be placed here. Even if it's just for 1-2 days. Including salary	Any funds in this offset will reduce the interest you pay on your O-Occ home loan
Equity Release LoanNo.1 RiverSt to be used for investment purposes	-$100,000 usually IO variable	Linked	EquityRelease OffsetNo.1 +$100,000	Same as example 1
Equity Release LoanNo.2 WindAve to be used for investment purposes	-$100,000 usually IO variable	Linked	EquityRelease OffsetNo.2 +$100,000	Same as example 1
Investment Property No1.River StLoan	-$500,000 can be P+I or IO (variable or fixed)		No offset is required as this is fully tax deductible	

Investment Property No2.Wind AveLoan	-$500,000 can be P+I or IO (variable or fixed)		No offset is required as this is fully tax deductible	

Note: It is vital to name each account according to its purpose and the property it secures. Same with the offset accounts. This will allow you to distinguish your loans and your offset amounts easily and will make tax time a breeze as you will know exactly how much interest you have paid for each account for each property.

Investment Tip # 8 - Who's your best friend? EQUITY!!! Your Tax-Free Bestie!

If you want to kick start your investment journey, then contact one of our team to discuss how you can make the most of your Equity Advantage.

4

CREATING AN INVESTMENT STRATEGY

When it comes to property investment strategies, there are many out there, and I'm sure you have heard of many yourself. I've seen and used many of them and helped finance many more. Let's run through a few:

- Negative Gearing/Capital Growth

- Positive Cash Flow

- Subdivisions

- P+I compounding

- 10 for every loan

- Duplex builds

- Buy a house with a large block, subdivide, build a new house, sell the existing property, keep the new property

- Subdivision/strata title duplexes

- Tax minimisation

- Weekly Tax up-front Strategy

- Buying New

- Renovating and holding

- Flipping (renovating and selling)

- Airbnb

- Cosmetic reno - Flipping

- Cosmetic reno - Holding

And the list goes on. To begin to decipher what type of strategy you should use can be determined by these three things:

1. Your risk profile: Click on the link for an example of a free risk profile test to see where you stand. Risk Profile Survey or go to www.opfinance.com.au/risk-profile-survey

2. What is it you want to achieve? What is your end goal?

Is it to buy three properties to pass on to your children to give them a helping hand?

Is it to build a multimillion-dollar portfolio that you can use to retire early?

Or to donate more to charity? Or to have a large passive income to add to your Super through retirement?

Is it to build a portfolio that will be the basis for developing generational wealth that will see your grandchildren's children looked after?

3. What is your borrowing capacity and what size is your deposit now and in the future?

Once you have these three requirements figured out, write them in the section below.

1

_____

_____

2

_____

_____

3

_____

_____

Let's say Person A, has a risk profile that shows you are an aggressive risk taker with a goal to build a retirement-level portfolio in 10 years and a borrowing capacity of $2,000,000 with a large deposit or equity.

Person B has a low-risk profile with a goal of buying properties in their price range to provide a modest passive income. Person B has a BC of $600,000 with a smaller deposit.

Person A may choose an Airbnb strategy as the rental yields can be very large, however, the risks are also increased due to the entry cost of a good Airbnb property and the potential for local and state rules to change and affect your ability to rent your property as you planned.

Another higher risk option for Person A could be to choose the 'Negative Gearing' strategy: purchase 3 high-value properties in blue-chip inner-city suburbs. Pay them down using the P+I compounding method and then sell one property to pay off the remaining two properties.

Person A would end up with a multi-million-dollar portfolio while only owning two investment properties. We will go into a full-length detailed breakdown of multiple scenarios in chapter 18.

Person B may choose the 'Buy New' strategy and purchase 1 new property for $600,000 in a regional area with a population of more than 50,000 with two or three main industries. In 3 years, they release equity and buy two more. And in another three years, they buy two more. Person B has purchased properties ranging from $450,000 to $600,000 while using equity to use as deposits.

They release the equity when it has accumulated and can stretch their BC by using 2nd and 3rd tier lenders to allow them to round out their portfolio. Person B has 5 properties worth $3.8m after 10 years.

They have earned higher yields (rental income) due to purchasing lower value properties, which have covered their repayments with no expenditure out of Person B's own pocket.

Person B may then sell their most expensive property to pay down some of the debt on the remaining 4 properties.

Two completely different strategies, though both have achieved their desired outcome while still meeting their risk profiles. There is no point in becoming a property investor if you can't sleep at night.

When you have chosen a strategy, a risk profile, and know your borrowing capacity, along with having a deposit, you can create your 'Buying Requirements' list. Your buying requirements are guidelines that you use to help you purchase the type of property that meets the area's demographic needs- as a place to live- and that fits your strategy and BC so that it will make a great first addition to your property portfolio.

For example, your buying requirements might be:

1. Looking for a property to renovate and hold.

2. BC is $750,000, so the property must be below $852,000. (88% of the purchase price)

3. In a regional city close to schools and a hospital, with a population of 50,000+.

4. 3 bedrooms, 2 baths and 1 car: You have spoken to local real estate property managers and found out that they are the most sought-after rental properties in that area.

5. The property must have cosmetic potential that can be addressed and renovated within your budget.

6. Rent for the property must achieve a 4.5% yield after the renovation.

7. The property should be over 550 square meters for future development potential on the rear of the block.

8. The vacancy rate in the area must be below 2.0%.

9. Should have close to a 30% demographic of renters in the suburb/town.

The above is an example of a detailed list of buying requirements that an investor might use, though they will be dependent on your strategy and your own financial situation.

You now have your strategy guidelines ticked off and all your buying requirements in place. You are ready for the next step. Researching your property.

Jump onto our website and take the Risk Profile Survey to see where you land at www.opfinance.com.au

---

Investment Tip # 4 – Only invest within your risk tolerance range.

5

FINANCE - WITHOUT FINANCE, YOU CAN'T EVEN BEGIN.

This is the second most important chapter of the whole book!

Let's go back a step or two and discuss how and when you should begin the process of getting your finance/loan/pre-approval.

Let's look at a few things we have to have in order prior to applying for a loan.

Living expenses: Try to have at least three months of clean, clear bank transactions. If you apply for a loan and your bank transactions show a lot of purchases from the pub every evening and sports bet deductions, then it does not look good in the bank's eyes.

Check your credit file and ensure it is clean and has no errors on it. Over 40% of credit files are found to have at least one mistake on them.

If you have recently paid off a credit card. Keep the closure letter to prove to the bank as the card will show up on your credit file for 3 – 6 months after.

If you are self-employed (SE), you will need to speak to your broker 12 months prior should you need a certain BC for your next purchase.

As a SE investor, just breaking even – so you don't pay any tax – does not make for an attractive loan application. You will need to show you have earned income, and the more, the better.

And yes, you will pay tax on that. That's the cost of a higher BC, which allows you to buy a higher-quality property. SE borrowers have the advantage that they can adjust their income through minimising deductions or increasing revenue if they have a target income they need to achieve for the year.

Now that both groups have spoken to their broker, at least a few months out, and have clean credit files and clean accounts, it's time to let your broker know you are ready to rock and roll.

They will go over all the details we have discussed. Your income, debt levels, LE, your goals now and in the future, your price range, repayment type, variable or fixed, ownership structure, and even if you want to use an environmentally conscious lender.

Your broker will then run an assessment against the lenders on their panel (usually 30 – 40 different lenders) and return some preferred options to the customer.

A point to note is that since the Banking Royal Commission, brokers are now legislated to work "in the client's best interests". Not the banks.

The banks are NOT required to have your best interest at heart. They can offer you a product that fails to meet your requirements, and they are completely protected.

They can offer you a higher interest rate than what they can actually get and receive a bonus for saving the bank money. Brokers will bend over backwards to get you a great result for your financial needs.

Virtually all the banks pay the same commissions, so brokers are not incentivised to send you to any particular bank.

So, choosing one lender over another generally comes down to suitability for the client's current financial situation, interest rate, and processing time, along with several specific policy niches if there are some non-standard aspects to the loan.

The broker will talk you through the selection and assist with any questions you might have.

If you need to release equity from an existing property to use as a deposit, then this is also the time to do it, as doing three loans is just as easy as doing one.

You will then have to present certain documents to prove your income, your debts, your children, and even who you are.

You will need to visually meet your broker, either in person or online, and you will need to sign documents for the application and acknowledge you have received certain pieces of vital information.

Your loan is submitted, and off it goes to the bank. Through the ether it travels until it reaches an assessor. They examine your application and documents and check them against the bank's policies. Sometimes, they will ask for more clarification from the client via the broker.

If you are doing an A, B, & C, then your refinance and equity release will be formally approved at the same time as your pre-approval is pre-approved.

Your pre-approval is valid for 3 to 6 months, depending on the lender. Once your equity release is formally approved, and your pre-approval is good to go, you can now begin your property hunt.

If you need more convincing on why to use a broker over going direct to bank, then please contact us at Open Plan Finance. We are more than happy to prove to you how we have your best interests at heart. If we can help you succeed, then we succeed.

Investment Tip # 5 –Finance is your make or break. Finding a mortgage broker/finance broker that is an experienced investor is vital. You want someone that knows both sides of the fence.

6

WHY AUSTRALIA'S PROPERTY MARKETS HAVE PERFORMED SO WELL FOR THE LAST 70 YEARS AND WILL PROBABLY CONTINUE TO DO SO

Australia has a love affair with property. They love reading about properties, watching record-breaking auctions of properties, watching renovations of properties, learning how to invest in property and how to buy and sell property.

We love the sea change, the tree change, and the big backyard with a barbie.

Thanks to COVID, there has been a real emphasis on the larger backyard and space to move in the last 24 months.

For 70 years, Australian house prices have gone up a lot and then gone down a little, over and over again.

Australia's trillion-dollar property market is the biggest industry in Australia. When the pandemic hit, the government was terrified of a property slump and threw bucketloads of money at the building industry. They did this as the real estate industry can get the economy moving quicker than any other.

Time and again, the government, banks, and in particular, the owners of properties themselves have helped keep this trend going.

It's almost as if we inherently know at a bone marrow level that if prices go down for a little bit, they will always go back up, and to even higher record levels than before.

When prices are dropping, most people don't freak out and sell; they take their properties off the market and wait. Then when the markets pick up again, they re-list and make a profit.

It's this innate knowledge and behaviour that helps protect Australia's property markets.

No one can say if this will continue. But one thing is for sure - the two drivers of an economy are demand and purchasing power. In a country like Australia, where we have one of the highest living standards in the world, we have a lot of purchasing power. And the demand to buy is huge.

Supply-side issues like local government red tape, tradie shortages, material shortages, and the big one, land shortages, do nothing but increase the demand for property.

If people feel they can't get a product that they want, then the demand goes up. With the housing supply shortage in Australia approaching emergency levels, even with interest rates rising faster than ever before in history, it has not dulled the appetite for Australian property.

Smart buyers know that massive wealth can be created when the masses are fearful and are on the hunt for a bargain. And they are out there. Immigration in Australia is about to be increased again, and there will soon be 300,000 new Australians wanting to find somewhere to live. Add this to the 100,000 new first-home buyers that enter the market each year, and the drivers are all there to keep property prices increasing for a very long time.

In the below graph, the 1950s was when price growth took off. It was in that period that immigration really picked up, and most of the 'sought-after' land around Sydney and Melbourne was taken.

Australian house prices
Inflation adjusted, March 2011 = 100*

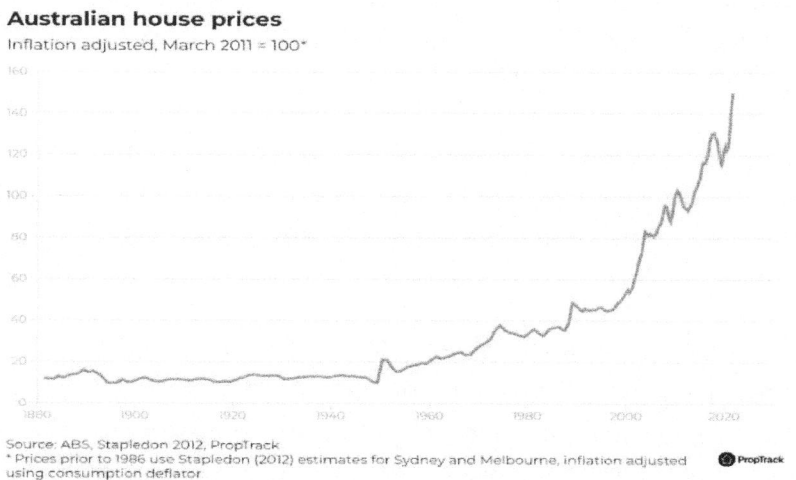

Source: ABS, Stapledon 2012, PropTrack
* Prices prior to 1986 use Stapledon (2012) estimates for Sydney and Melbourne, inflation adjusted using consumption deflator

In 1989, property prices spiked again due to the deregulation of the finance industry, the floating of the Australian dollar, and credit becoming a lot easier to obtain.

As you can see, the Australian government realises that the housing industry is its most important industry. It is a ten trillion-dollar industry that employs more of Australia's citizens than any other.

From the banks to the tradies, to the real estate agents, the mortgage brokers, the solicitors/conveyancers, property managers, property investors, investment educators, financial advisers, accountants, construction companies, land developers, valuers, surveyors, quantity surveyors, property investment journalists, property investment podcasters, draftsman, architects, and all the office staff to manage these businesses.

When COVID hit, the first thing the government did was to offer a Home Builder scheme to inject more money into the housing industry. It is routinely said that the housing industry is a protected industry, and many believe the Australian housing industry is too big to fail.

In 2008 when the GFC wiped out entire countries, Australia held firm. Some say it was due to the government backing the major banks, so there wasn't a "run on the banks" like in other countries.

I think that it's more to do with the psychology that Australian homeowners have, which I'll go into a little later. During that meltdown, we were lucky enough that our banks didn't have as much invested in subprime mortgages as other countries. So a small 10% correction was all we saw in the worst-hit suburbs. Some suburbs plateaued for 18 months and then took off again, seeing between 15-33% growth from 2009-2011.

One analysis of data by Domain showed that over the last 30 years, house prices increased on average for 33 months, and prices rose by an average of 32.7% each time. While the downward cycle lasted only nine months, and the decrease in national prices was only 3%.

This statistic may be getting a nudge at the moment, though, even at a record-breaking drop in house prices of 15%, which is being predicted by some economists. Even then, it's of virtually little consequence to the overall market. Let me explain this statement.

Many people put their properties on the market to be sold in mid-2022, hoping that the large prices obtained during the previous year would continue. They did not, and many of those properties were subsequently pulled from the market. The sellers know that if they wait, prices will go back up. They are in no hurry.

When an entire market knows that prices will increase again, it adds a whole other level of psychology to the market. And it adds a resilience that I believe few markets have in other parts of the world. Maybe New York and in some areas of Canada, but very few others.

People that would be affected by a 15% decrease are people that for whatever reason, HAVE to sell their property. These people may miss out on a small portion of profits.

Owner-occupiers that have no requirement to sell or release equity will not be affected by a 15% decrease in the national market. This portion of the market is around 60%. So, large amounts of homeowners are not affected if property prices drop slightly.

If you are looking to renovate and need to release equity to do it, then you may be slightly affected, but on the whole, there are not many people adversely affected by property prices taking a nap for a year or two.

First Home Buyers may end up in a negative equity situation. This is when the amount owing on your property is more than its value. But again, it's of no real issue if you have no plans to sell. If you can cover the repayments, then going into negative equity for 12-18 months is of no real concern.

Many property commentators like to claim Australia has only one property market. That's not true. It actually has over 30 different markets, and they are not all affected by the same fluctuations at the same time and to the same extent. When Sydney and Melbourne's prices take a nosedive (like it's doing now), areas like Brisbane or Perth continue to increase.

If you diversify your portfolio through location, then you have effectively de-risked your investment. Putting all your eggs in one state basket can add extra risk that you, as an investor, can minimise by investing in multiple states.

There is a term in Value Investing called a "Moat." This is a company's competitive advantage over the competition and helps protect it from competitors. As a property investor, your Moat is the location of your property.

Investment Tip #6 – A capital loss on property can be carried forward indefinitely, until you make a capital gain.

7

CASH FLOW OR CAPITAL GROWTH

This one will keep you up at night. There are still very strong arguments for cash flow. And just as strong for capital growth. And there is a strong case to be made for trying to obtain both. In fact, if you can achieve both, then you have the best of both worlds.

If you cannot have both, then which one is better?

Let's start with cash flow and what it is as an investment strategy.

Cash flow means that your investment property is making a profit. That at the end of the financial year after all expenses like council rates, insurance and interest on your loan, you have cash left over. Be aware that you will also pay tax on that profit.

There are two types of Cash flow:

Positive Geared Cash Flow: That's a profit after you receive your tax return. Your tax refund pushes your property's profit and loss for the year to a profit.

The other is **Cash Flow Positive-** That's when your investment is making profit even before you complete your tax return. Your rental return is covering your repayments and expenses each month.

To use cash flow as an investment, you must have a property that is costing you less every month through mortgage repayments, property management costs, insurance, and council rates vs the rent you are receiving.

Cash flow properties are usually found in regional areas where there is a lack of rental accommodation and relatively cheap properties to buy. This causes tenants to have to pay a higher amount in rent compared to the cost of the property. Cash flow positive strategies can also be created by dual occupancy builds or purchases.

Many times, adding a granny flat or building a duplex will create enough rental income to cover all your investment costs.

People use a cash flow strategy to increase their income, get into a market that may see capital growth in the future, and increase their Borrowing Capacity (BC). If your income does not increase over time, then as you buy more properties, your debt level increases, and eventually, you will hit the financial brick wall. You won't be able to borrow any more money, which means your investment journey is at an end. Though, by continually increasing your income through a cash flow strategy your BC is likely to keep increasing, and you can keep buying property. Cash Flow properties should achieve a 6% yield or higher.

If you are handy or can organise trades well, doing a cosmetic renovation of a cheaper property can increase its value and allow you to charge higher rents to your tenants. This can help turn your negative geared property into a cash flow machine.

Capital Growth: This strategy usually relies on you waiting for the market to go up or creating value, for example, through a renovation. When using capital growth as a strategy, your properties will most likely be negatively geared and will be costing you 'cash' each month as the rent received will not be enough to cover your investment costs.

Why would people do this? Because while you are subsidising your investment, your investment is increasing in value due to its location and the increasing demand for properties of its type. Often, your property can increase in value far exceeding any rent you could charge each week.

During one of the market's upswings, one of our properties went up $200,000 in 6 months. That's the equivalent of a $7,692 increase in value every week for six months. In the 2021 – 2022 price boom, some properties have doubled in value in 18 months.

Those sorts of massive capital increases are almost non-existent in other forms of assets. Certainly, no cash flow positive property can hope to achieve that kind of result.

Now, to be fair, a doubling of value is not a realistic goal in such a short period, though seeing a 20% increase in one year can and does often happen if you have purchased well and the economic and social drivers are there to promote growth.

When researching Capital Growth areas look for year-on-year growth of above 5% and closer to 10% if possible.

Many people still believe that price growth is derived from Supply and Demand. But in fact, they are just two sides of the same coin. High supply; there will be less demand which will lead to less supply which will increase demand and increase supply, and so on.

But your capacity to buy is one of the key drivers of capital and economic growth. If you can't afford a house, then no amount of supply or demand will change that.

Think about a new hospital opening in a suburb that previously was predominately a lower-income area. Nurses, doctors, and anesthesiologists are now looking to live close to work and bring with them large borrowing capacities.

They can and are willing to pay more for properties, therefore, pushing house prices in that area up. Borrowing Capacity is the little brother to the Investment God "Equity."

Investment Tip #7 — If your income is restricting your Borrowing Capacity, then focus on Cash Flow properties initially.

8

WHERE TO START

Budget + Living Expenses

Most people would be aware of what a budget is and how it is theoretically supposed to operate. You set yourself an amount of money to spend each week or month, and you only spend that amount. The remainder/leftover is put aside to go towards whatever goal you had budgeted for in the first place. It's pretty simple.

Yet, it's surprising how many people cannot and will not stick to a budget. I have seen thousands of budgets, and maybe 1% was an accurate representation of 'people spending.'

As you build your portfolio, you will need to learn to budget. Hopefully, that habit will remain, but on the other hand, you can't be so restrictive you are living on 2-minute noodles and toast. Set yourself an amount of 'spending money' – your 'fun money' that you have set aside in cash and stick to it.

Saving for your deposit will be the one time when your budgeting may need to remain tight for a few years and, hopefully, no more than five.

Saving for a deposit is hard. You should only have to save for one deposit in your life. So, the really hard yards of budgeting only need to be travelled once.

The only other time you may need to keep your budgeting tight is for three months before your loan application.

What is a Living Expense (LE)? From a bank's perspective, let's face it; when you are building a property portfolio, the banks are the only people you need to impress.

So from a bank's perspective, living expenses are your everyday expenses. These include groceries, fuel, council rates, water rates, medical expenses, public school fees, and entertainment.

Discretionary expenses are things like daycare fees, private school fees, and health insurance. Discretionary expenses can be assessed at a higher rate than everyday expenses. Why a person paying private health insurance is negatively affected in the bank's eyes is a mystery to me, but to some banks it does.

If your living expenses are within the average band for an individual or family of your size, in your postcode, and for your income level, then the banks are happy. If they are higher than average, the banks are even happier because that shows an accurate awareness of your spending.

However, if they are lower than the average HEMS (Household Expenditure Measure), the bank's 'spider senses' prickle, and they start to take a closer look. They think you can't accurately calculate your expenses.

Yes, you read that correctly. The bank thinks you manage money better if you use a higher-than-average monthly budget.

And they think you are poor at managing money if you indicate a budget under what they have assessed your average to be. It seems counter-intuitive, but that's the system we have to work with.

Hopefully, you are just part of the 1% that can budget effectively, and everything is fine. Though most times, the bank will see that there have been expenses missed, and a client is unaware of the actual amount they spend each month.

This can be another red flag to a lender.

When it comes to budgeting and living expenses, make sure your LE is clean for at least three months before your loan application.

By clean, I mean no expenditures on a large or frivolous item and definitely, no gambling or large cash withdrawals from the local pub ATM (use the one down the road).

Bad debt

To answer what bad debt is, we need to understand what good debt is.

Good debt is the debt you have on something that increases in value or creates income for you. These are called assets. Assets are good. A debt against assets is ok, too; hence the term 'good debt.'

So, if you have a loan for a property, that is classed as good debt.

Same with shares and bonds. If they grow in value or return a dividend, then they are classed as an asset and are, therefore, 'good debt.'

Bad debt is anything else. Credit cards, personal loans, car loans, HELP debt, Zip pay, and After pay.

Don't get stuck on the term 'Bad.' Just think of them as 'not helping your borrowing capacity.'

For every $1,000 credit card limit, the bank will reduce your borrowing capacity by $4,000. So, if you have a $25,000 'emergency' credit card sitting around that you have never used, that card is reducing your borrowing capacity by $100,000. If you want to be a property investor, get rid of it!

An easy way of increasing a person's borrowing capacity is to reduce his/her bad debt. Sometimes, we can release equity to pay off the bad debt to allow servicing to PASS for a loan.

Interestingly, you can use 'equity,' which is released through more debt, to pay off a different type of debt, and it will improve your Borrowing Capacity (BC). It goes to show how detrimental bad debt can be to your financial health.

I have seen people with $150,000 of maxed-out credit card debt, and it is extremely hard for an individual to climb out of that much debt.

As a rule, I would put a limit on yourself and have no more than two bad debts against your name or a family unit at one time.

For example, one car loan and a small $5,000 credit card to use in an emergency. That should be the absolute maximum amount of bad debt you carry. Never max out your credit card, and don't EVER go over your credit card limit. This will show up on your bank statements which potential lenders will see now that comprehensive credit reporting is operating between all banks.

Income: How much is enough?

That all depends on what your goals are and what you want to buy. If you want to buy a $1,000,000 property and are single and earn $50,000 a year, and have a $40,000 car loan, I'm afraid you are out of luck.

Your income is one part of a four-part equation when it comes to borrowing capacity. They interact with each other in the following way:

Income Vs Debt + (LE & dependants) = Borrowing Capacity

Although the actual Borrowing Capacity calculation is not as simple as the above formula.

It is quite complex, and each lender has their own policies and algorithms to work them out. As for how they interact, it's basically your income VS your debt. And yes, the number of children and how much you spend each month are added to your debt.

Your income is relatively straightforward.

Let's unpack each type- For PAYG earners. It is the annual amount you earn GROSS PAYG plus a percentage of your overtime and bonuses. It's usually 80 – 100% of OT, and the lowest amount of your bonus paid over the last two years. For example in one year, you earn $100,000 gross PAYG and have performed $10,000 of OT and have been receiving a $5,000 bonus every year for over two years. The income most banks will allow in servicing is $100,000 + $8,000 + $5,000 for a total of $113,000.

For the Self-Employed, it is the NET PROFIT BEFORE TAX (NPBT) that your business has made. If you have paid yourself a wage, then you can add the NPBT and the wage you have paid yourself to get the total income amount the bank will use for your assessment. We can add depreciation and interest paid on business loans as income also.

WARNING! I see this so much; it hurts, and it is amazing that accountants still recommend this strategy to small business owners.

If you run a small business, either as a sole trader or as a company, DO NOT purposely try to NOT PAY any tax by only just making a small profit or making a small loss. It's ridiculous to think that by trying to save on tax, you will run up your business's expenses to a point where you actually have no profit.

What if you pay yourself a wage, I hear you say? Well, great. If your business makes a $10,000 loss, but you've paid yourself $60,000 throughout the year. Guess what? Most banks will say you only earned $50,000.

As a starting point, every business owner should pay themselves up front every week, fortnight or month. Then, pay your expenses with what is left over.

If you can't afford your expenses, then you need to lower your expenses. It's simple. Refer to a great book called 'Profit First' for the full breakdown of how a small business can implement this simple process to start making cash flow and profit a regular occurrence.

If you want to build a multi-million-dollar property portfolio, then you will need to show very strong self-employed income, preferably over two years. For PAYG earners, it's a little easier as you only need to be in full or part-time permanent work for two weeks, and you can get a loan with most major banks.

Yes, that means that you, the employee, may be approved for a loan while your employer may get rejected for a loan, even though they are the source of your income.

So, going back to the Income Vs Debt calculation, we have now clarified what income is.

We know what debt is.

The other smaller components that do slightly change your borrowing capacity are your living expenses (LE), which we have discussed, and the final piece, how many dependents you have. Three kids are going to mean your borrowing capacity is less than a person on the same income and debt levels that only has one child.

As a summary of the income question for Self Employed (SE), I personally focused on my SE income for 12 months prior to purchasing more property.

I spoke to a broker (myself); I calculated what my current BC was; I estimated what type of properties I wanted to buy in 12 months, and then, I set a goal to be able to show that amount of income in the next year's tax return.

The point is- for self-employed investors, you need to be looking at least 12 months ahead to maximise what you can achieve. Some brokers can't handle the complexities of self employed financials though at Open Plan Finance we love them.

For PAYG employees, it may be a case of working a lot of OT (Over Time) over 12 months to boost your income.

And that's all I have to say about Income. 😊

Deposit

Deposit is the final piece of the purchasing power equation. Your deposit is not directly correlated to your borrowing capacity, but it is vitally important to your purchasing power.

Let's say Joe and Jackie earn $500,000 a year each; they have no children, and they have no debt.

Now, their borrowing capacity is going to be exceedingly high- around $7,000,000 actually; however, they have $0 savings, so they have no deposit. Therefore, they can't afford to purchase a property.

Now, the connection between BC and Deposit becomes clearer. You need both BC and Deposit to be able to purchase a property. You can't have one without the other and still purchase a property.

Your deposit can come in many forms: savings, equity, parental gift, or a parental guarantee.

Savings: is pretty self-explanatory. You save your butt off over many years and use those funds as your deposit.

Now we are into the good stuff!

Equity: is usually the preferred source of a deposit for an investor. Equity is your investment gold! Equity is the difference between what your property is valued at and the remaining loan on that property.

For example, your property is valued at $1,000,000, and you have $500,000 still owing. Your equity is therefore $500,000. But you can't use all that equity. The banks always like to keep some skin in the game and will only allow you to access equity from 80% of the value of your home without paying lenders' mortgage insurance.

So, of the $500,000 in equity, the bank will allow you to borrow $300,000. Keeping 20% of the value as their buffer. E.g. $1,000,000 X 0.8 - $500,000 = $300,000

The correct way to use your equity for a deposit is to release it as a separate loan with an offset account.

Equity of amounts larger than $60,000 that are going to be used for investment should be released as an Interest Only (IO) variable loan with an offset.

Why? So you are not paying interest on the loan until you use it?

In the example above, that would be a $300,000 Interest Only loan with an offset account. The $300,000 in funds is deposited into the offset account linked to the equity loan of $300,000. While those two amounts are equally balanced, you won't make any repayments.

If your IO term is 5 years, as most are, then you can theoretically keep that $300,000 on hand for five years and never have to make a repayment on the borrowed money.

Parental Gift: Saving for a deposit is hard. Add in rent and increased living expenses with minimal wage growth, and it can feel like banging your head against a wall.

If your parents or a close relative have the funds, then they can gift you the funds for a deposit. Many banks will accept this with a letter stating that the funds are a 'non-refundable gift.' This won't necessarily guarantee your approval.

The bank needs to ensure that you can cover the mortgage repayment, so it will weigh up what your rental expenses are per month and add what you have been able to save per month. If this is approximately what your mortgage will cost, then you should be fine.

Parental Guarantee: This is the least popular option and for a good reason. Parental guarantees are when your parents stake a portion of the equity of their property as a deposit. Usually, 20%.

Essentially, they are putting a second mortgage on their property. I'm not a fan of this strategy as it puts the parents, who are usually approaching retirement age, in a risky situation where they can be held responsible for their child's mortgage if they fail to make repayments. Some lenders will require the parents' property to be refinanced over to the new bank that their child is using, which can be a considerable time waster if a purchase has time frame deadlines that need to be met.

It also adds to increased payments for the applicant (You) receiving the parental guarantee.

As the loan is separated into two splits—an 80% split and a 20% split. The repayments on both splits must be paid by the applicants. The parents are not required to make any payments.

Their 20% is only a paper transfer, and a 'caveat' is placed on their property (if the property was not refinanced), saying that another lender has some stake in their property.

With a normal purchase, a person's loan might be anything from 90% or less of the purchase price. With a parental guarantee, you will be covering 100% of the borrowings and making repayments on 100% of the cost of the property.

Of all the different types of deposits, equity is by far the preferred option. It gives you the Equity Advantage.

It's tax-free, it's easy to access, and you can increase your equity just by obtaining a higher valuation.

What's that, you say?

That's right; the amount of equity is determined by your property's valuation; however, a valuation is just a valuer's opinion, and as you well know, many people have differing opinions.

I have seen valuations differ up to $200,000 on the same property. That's an extra $160,000 in equity just by getting a second valuation that came back higher. Now that's an Equity Advantage.

I truly believe the main benefit of using equity is that it is using 'other people's money.' Yes, you could use your savings, but you have struggled for years to build those savings and paid tax on them.

Why not use other people's money and leverage their cash to increase your wealth?

If you have a gun team of property experts already lined up to help, your property journey becomes much easier.

Investment Tip #8 – Car loans kill people's borrowing capacity more than any other type of debt. Speak to a finance consultant before you take out a car loan if you plan on investing in property so that you don't unintentionally set yourself back years.

9

WHAT IS YOUR PRICE RANGE?

A person's price range is going to be dependent on their investment strategy, their deposit/equity and borrowing capacity.

If a person has a huge borrowing capacity and $500,000 for deposit, then their price range will be dependent on the type of property they wish to buy.

If they are 'borrowing capacity and deposit-dependent' as most people are, then it will come down to what you can afford and trying to obtain your goals while working within your BC and deposit restrictions.

An example is a client who has $300,000 of equity released to use for deposits. Their borrowing capacity is very high, so in this instance, it's only a matter of how to distribute those funds to each purchase.

In this case, they want to buy two properties with their $300,000 of equity. The first property will be around the $850,000 price range.

To maximise their equity funds, they will be making 12% deposits for both properties. A 12% deposit on an $850,000 purchase is $102,000. Add in Stamp Duty (SD) of $28,000, and they will be using around $130,000 of their $300,000.

Their second purchase is of a lesser value property of $700,000. A 12% deposit will be $84,000 and an SD of $20,000. So, a total of $104,000.

All up, they have now used $234,000 of their $300,000 equity, with $66,000 remaining.

For a person that has saved their first deposit and has no equity to rely on, then they will usually be dependent on the amount of deposit saved. This will be the major factor in what you can afford once your borrowing capacity is established.

Luckily, the current property industry in Australia has many different government schemes and stamp duty (SD) exemptions to assist first-time homebuyers (FHB).

Each state has grants for FHB that purchase a new property, offering anywhere between $10,000 and $30,000.

Each state has various Stamp Duty or Transfer Tax Exemptions that can potentially eliminate having to pay for Stamp Duty.

However, these limits are very outdated and really only applicable in certain regional areas and outer suburbs to be able to take full advantage of them due to the cost of property in metro areas.

The First-Home Loan Deposit scheme introduced by the previous government will allow FHBs earning between $120,000 (singles) or $180,000 (for couples) to purchase a new property using only a 5% deposit. No LMI is required, and you get lower interest rates as if you had paid a 20% deposit.

Another 30,000 of these spots have just become available as of the 1st of July 2022. This scheme has been widened again as of the writing of this book and now the eligibility requirements are even more relaxed. First Home Buyers should definitely look into it.

The new 2023 Labor government also has a scheme where you can purchase a property with only a 2% deposit, and the government will 'acquire' 35% (or 40% if new), meaning you must only make repayments on the 65% or 60% of the purchase price. The government will retain any capital growth of its share.

You can purchase the remaining amount back from the government if and when you can. This scheme is only offered through one bank and the eligibility requirements are very strict.

There is also the Family Home Deposit scheme for single parents that allows you to purchase with only a 2% deposit.

I don't particularly rate this scheme as most applicants are divorced or separated applicants who are not eligible for the FHB scheme as they had purchased with their ex-spouse, meaning they still have to pay full stamp duty. Full stamp duty on any house above $500,000 is almost as much as the 2% deposit they had saved negating most of the benefit.

Now these schemes and grants are only for FHB and can't be used by investors. So if you are looking to get onto the property ladder and buy your own home, these are a great way to get a leg up.

If you are unsure if you qualify for one of the above spots, then speak to one of our team. We are experts on maximising these government benefits.

Investment Tip #9 – When using one of the above government schemes, you may only have to live in the property for 12-24 months in some cases before you can switch the property to an investment and charge rent. ☺

10

BUYING YOUR FIRST PROPERTY

Ahh, the giant leap into the unknown. Purchasing your first property can be one of the scariest actions you ever take. But you need to take it. Getting your foot in the door, so to speak, is essential. The earlier, the better.

There is a saying in the property industry that goes, 'When is the best time to buy an investment property? The answer is 20 years ago.'

'So, when is the second-best time to buy an investment property? Well, the answer to that is today!' And that principle is still so very true.

Now, you can time the market, and honestly, if you buy in the next 12 months, you will actually have timed the market, but I'll show you how that is still irrelevant.

For reference, it is currently May 2023. Trying to time the market has cost tens of thousands of Australians tens of millions of dollars in capital growth over the last 20 years because they never took the leap and bought.

Whether you buy at the dip or at the peak is irrelevant as long as you get into the market. If your BC and deposit will only allow you to buy a $200k property, then do that. Rent for another few years if you must. Just getting into the market is how you start to use your Equity Advantage and fast track your way to a retirement-level portfolio!

Now I know rents are going off the deep end in 2023, and it's extremely expensive to rent where you want to live.

My advice is to live further away than you want to. Yes, that sucks, but it is necessary so that you do not reduce your BC by spending too much of your income on rent.

To build a retirement-level portfolio, you will need to make some sacrifices, and living further away from the CBD or your work so that your rent is cheaper is one way. Lower rent means you can save up a deposit faster.

As a first-time buyer, an Owner Occupier or as an investor, your deposit will most likely be your biggest hurdle, it can take years to save for a deposit, so if you have determined that your income is a limiting factor in your goal, then you have time to retrain to earn more or request a raise.

To continue to invest, I know some clients that have retrained and left their entire profession behind to earn more so they could continue investing. This kind of awareness and dedication to reaching one's goals is truly admirable. And shows a true understanding of the Equity Advantage of using the current system and your own determination to reach your long-term goals.

If you are reading this book, then you have taken that first step and have the determination. Now you just need to learn the steps to continue climbing the property ladder.

The Loan process:

So many people, even those that have bought multiple properties, have limited knowledge of the loan process. Even many sales agents only have a limited understanding of the loan process.

See below for your 20-step guide from starting a budget to popping the champagne on your first property:

1. Set your budget and begin the process of saving or have a heart-to-heart with your parents to see if they will 'gift' you some funds.

2. While you are saving, do some research on what some of the commonly used terms are, which the bank and real estate agents will use, and you have to know i.e., LVR, LMI, equity, and deposit.

3. About 1 year out from purchasing, have your income assessed by a mortgage broker to see what areas you need to focus on leading up to your application.

4. Once you have your deposit sorted and your BC is high enough to purchase the type of property you want, then it's time to knuckle down.

5. Stick to three months of keeping to your budget, the banks may want to see your expenditure over the last 90 days, so keep it clean in case they do.

6. Speak to your broker 3 months out and have them determine which lender, loan product, and financial fit will suit your needs and achieve your goals.

7. Apply for a pre-approval up to your maximum amount using the agreed-upon deposit percentage. By this, I mean if it's advised to make a 12% deposit, then 12% should be what all your calculations are based on.

8. It works like this- You and the broker have determined that a 12% deposit is preferable because it saves you $8,000 in LMI by staying under 90% LVR. The bank has pre-approved you for a loan of $528,000 for a purchase price of $600,000.

   Your pre-approval will say you are pre-approved for a loan of $528,000, but that does not mean that if you buy a property for $550,000 ($50,000 below your original purchase price), the bank will still lend you $528,000. If your purchase price has decreased, then so does the amount the bank will lend you.

   In this scenario, the new loan amount would be 88% of $550,000, which is $484,000. Your 12% deposit is still 12%. It is now 12% of $550,000.

9. Your pre-approval is approved to your maximum amount. You should always go for the maximum, as reducing your loan is easy and can be done in seconds by the assessor.

   Increasing your loan amount will require a few days of assessment by the bank as they will need to go over all your information again and may ask for more bank statements and pay slips. Losing 2 – 3 days (in some cases, 7 – 10 days) can literally destroy your chances of securing a property. If there are tight time frames involved, such as 5-days cooling-off period, or the vendor is inflexible and won't extend your cooling-off period to achieve formal approval.

10. Contact a solicitor or conveyancer and have him/her talk you through the process from their end. They will be the ones to check any contracts and add any clauses you might want to include, along with advising on outstanding deposit amounts and where to transfer those funds.

11. You find a property, either yourself, using all the knowledge you have absorbed over the last few years saving for a deposit, or by using a buyer's agent, and you make an offer. The negotiations go back and forth, and eventually, your offer is accepted. Yeah!

12. Let your broker know ASAP. The sooner you let your broker know, the better. Once your offer is accepted, the clock starts. And yes, it is a race.

If the market is crazy hot like in 2021, then a 5-day cooling off (in NSW) or a very short finance clause may be all you get. During this time, you have to have had a valuation completed of your intended property, a building and pest inspection and obtain Formal Approval from your lender, who honestly does not care about your time constraints or how much you love the property. They will work at their own speed and not give your impending finance date a second thought.

13. This process can change a little, depending on which state you are in, but in most states, it goes like this-

Once you have an offer accepted, the sales agent will want you to come in and sign your Contract of Sale. Once this is signed, then the clock officially starts. But your broker can get a head start on the process by ordering the valuation before the contract is signed. Most valuers require a signed front page of the COS to order the valuation.

You, the buyer, can take a copy of the front page before the official signing, sign, and date it for the broker. This copy only ever goes to the valuer who doesn't care two hoots about it other than that it's signed, which means they can get their commission fee and start the valuation.

This can save you days in the valuation process. When you sign the official contract of sale, this should also be the time to finalise your insurance; as legally, in most states, you technically own the property from the date you sign, not the date the funds were transferred or the settlement date.

14. Having your pre-approval in order means the process to receive Formal Approval should be relatively fast. Getting that 'Formal Approval' email or call is an amazing feeling, particularly if you are down to the last few hours of your cooling-off period.

15. You are 'Formally Approved,' so you can celebrate but not too much. There is still the signing of the loan documents. Now, every bank has different loan documents, and they are all difficult to read. So, please, speak to your broker's Settlements Manager if you have any questions.

It's 100% better to get it right the first time rather than entering the wrong information or forgetting to enter a witness' address correctly to then have the bank tell you 3 days before settlement that your loan documents have not been completed correctly. This can and has caused many missed settlements and thousands of dollars in late fees to be paid by the buyer.

16. You return the loan documents and your (Certificate of Currency) COC and ensure that any remaining deposit funds are in your solicitor's account or in the account the bank has set up for you at least three days before settlement.

    With the rise in email scams, it's best to call your solicitor and confirm the account details over the phone. People have been duped of their entire home deposit when hackers have sent emails while posing as the person's solicitor and given account details of their own. A 2-minute phone call might save you $100,000 and a LOT of heartache.

17. Settlement occurs; your funds required are transferred to the seller by the solicitor, and the bank pays the remaining amount to the seller also. You receive the keys from the agent, and you pop the champagne.

18. If LMI is required, then the bank will add the LMI amount to your loan amount, set up your accounts and offsets, and will transfer any remaining funds into your nominated account.

19. It's vitally important to check that your loan accounts are set up and linked to the correct offset accounts. This can be done via the bank's online portal or by calling them.

    Often, banks will not link offset accounts, and clients can go many months without receiving the benefits of the funds in their offset accounts. If you can't do it online, you may need to call the lender to check. It's a pain; however, the broker, unfortunately, can't check to see if this is done. It's all back-end processed by the bank. And it is vital it is set up correctly for you to receive the benefit.

20. Rinse and repeat, but next time, you will use equity, not your savings. That will be the beginning of your Equity Advantage.

Your first repayment will be due after one month, and it is very important to make sure you have all your automated transfers or direct debits sorted so that no payments are missed.

As you can see the loan process can be very complicated and can drag on for months if you don't have a team of brokers with streamline processes. So do your research and find a good broker.

Investment Tip #10 – Take years off saving for your deposit by using one of the 5% or similar government schemes - and remember, you should only ever have to save a deposit once in your life.

11

DUE DILIGENCE

Where to start your investment property research? Well, if you use a buyer's agent or investment specialist, you won't have to carry out any of the research yourself.

However, I would recommend knowing how to find all the metrics, vacancy rates, historical capital growth rates, population numbers, suburb demographics, population movement figures, employment demographics, approved infrastructure projects and some local knowledge that a buyer's agent will provide.

Based on your strategy, risk profile and BC and having created your buying requirements, you now need to complete the Due Diligence (DD) process. Completing a thorough DD process will mean less chance of buyer's remorse from purchasing a dud property.

Property is not something that you should rush into. Nor should you become emotionally involved in any one particular property. That is certainly easier said than done, especially when you suddenly find the PERFECT property that meets all your buying requirements!

To find out where to find the below information for each vital category, just follow the link:

Vacancy rates: SQM-
https://sqmresearch.com.au/graph_vacancy.php

Historical growth rates: Your Investment Property Magazine
Yourinvestmentpropertymag.com.au

Bureau of Statistics for:

Population growth

Population movement
https://www.abs.gov.au/statistics/people/housing/housing-occupancy-and-costs/latest-release

Suburb demographics: Residex, Core Logic. Ask your Broker for these as they will have access to reports that will help your Due Diligence.

Population movement figures: Bureau of statistics-

https://www.abs.gov.au/statistics/people/housing/housing-occupancy-and-costs/latest-release

Employment demographics: Residex -
https://www.corelogic.com.au/software-solutions/rp-data?redirect=yes&utm_source=residex.com.au&utm_medium=referral&utm_campaign=residex-retirement

Core Logic –
https://www.corelogic.com.au/?gclid=Cj0KCQjwguGYBhDRARIsAHgRm49pKjTDz-ZPTVLBybJKJUIvxE43RiGl8mfKAwCK7p3JcBH7WyGwSqgaAuTnEALw_wcB

Bureau of statistics -

https://www.abs.gov.au/statistics/people/housing/housing-occupancy-and-costs/latest-release

Approved infrastructure projects-

https://www.infrastructureaustralia.gov.au/infrastructure-%20priority-list

Local Council websites.

Local Council Town Planners- A very valuable resource

Ok! So, now, you have all these great pieces of information, but why do you need them? Why do they matter and how do they help you to buy an incredible investment property?

Let's join the dots in the next chapter so that everything becomes clearer.

Investment Tip # 11 – Due Diligence is how you de-risk your investment. Remember your property's MOAT is its location. If you get that right, 70% of the work is done.

12

JOINING THE DOTS: HOW ALL THE PIECES OF THE PUZZLE FIT TOGETHER

Where do you start looking for a property?

www.realestate.com.au, right?

NO. But it's good fun window shopping there to get a feel of things. But let's back the truck up a little bit.

We have so far figured out your risk profile and what it is you hope to achieve; we know your borrowing capacity, and you have your deposit or equity, plus your pre-approval. You are ready. But where do you start?

This is where your strategy and buying requirements come into play. Your strategy will direct you to the type of property you want to buy.

Let's say your strategy is to 'Cosmetic Renovate and Hold.' Therefore, you will be looking at existing properties that need a little work that you can add value to with a fast renovation.

Your borrowing capacity will determine the value of the properties you can buy, so you will be focused within a specific price range. Obviously, that's what you are limited to or need to limit yourself to if your plan is to buy more than one great property in quick succession.

You will also need to be looking at where the markets are going now and are likely to go in the future. It is said that there are over 30 property markets in Australia, but mainstream media often says that there is only one Australian property market- which is ridiculous.

To think that property prices in Tasmania, with its own industry, development laws and culture will have the same peaks and valleys that Sydney property has is delusional. Take Brisbane for example; for 20 years it was supposed to be the next big boom city. And it just simmered away getting 4% growth with no major fluctuations up or down.

That is until the pandemic hit, and they won the 2032 Olympics. It has seen a lot more than 4% growth since then.

Sydney and Melbourne have certainly come off the boil; however, if buying in one of those cities is part of your strategy, then buying when the market is priced low in continuously cyclic growth markets like Sydney and Melbourne are, could be a great opportunity.

You may notice that I do not direct you to a particular strategy. That's because everyone has their own specific needs, and you might want to invest using multiple strategies over your investment life as your goals and priorities change. I know I have.

I've used cosmetic renovations, cash flow student accommodation, and capital growth/negative gearing as strategies during my time as an investor. Each chosen at a particular time to meet a particular need. You will most likely do the same.

Back to Joining the Dots

Start by looking at economic drivers like big infrastructure projects such as hospitals, airports, population migration, lifestyle features, and at the end of the day, price.

If there is a large price disparity in a place that has all this compared to a similar city that is already priced very high, then the signals are starting to indicate that there may be some investment opportunities there.

If there are locations in that state that match your buying rules, then that is a good place to start. Don't be limited to your own state. There are many ways you can protect yourself and your property with property managers and insurance so that you don't need to stand guard over your property by buying the house next door.

So, you have matched your borrowing capacity and pre-approval amount to a state and region that has good population migration and economic drivers.

Now, you need to find a specific area. Using the strategy above, the investor will want good capital growth if they are holding the property. The renovation will increase the rental yield, and getting sustained capital growth would be a key principle in making this strategy outperform many others.

One way to determine future capital growth is to look for historic capital growth. Many of the online free examples above will give you a pretty accurate breakdown of what a suburb's capital growth has been year on year for the last decade.

Now, there is always the disclaimer that previous capital growth is not a guarantee of future capital growth, but it can be a good indicator.

Mining towns are the exception. Just don't bother with them. One-industry towns are not a good investment. Same with towns/regional area with a population under 50,000. Why limit your rental base on purpose?

Approved government spending in the area, and if that area has some natural features that make it attractive or limits the number of properties that can be built, such as an ocean, cliffs or a mountain, then that can be a key factor in capital growth also.

Areas with large green belts where estates can be built usually don't see capital growth for at least 5 years. However, the pandemic has turned that on its head in some areas.

So, you have now found a suburb or group of suburbs in a particular state that has good growth potential due to meeting the criteria above. You have your price range determined by your BC, and you have a list of the items you are willing to renovate to add value. In this instance, nothing more than a kitchen, flooring, exterior paint and some minor landscaping.

But there is still a raft of hurdles that can pull you unstuck. For instance- what are the zoning and DA rules in that area? A great way to get an idea of what might and might not be allowed is to call the town planner. They are generally pretty agreeable and are happy to chat about proposed developments.

Even if they can't give you specifics or a firm 'Yes' for a particular property or scenario, they may point you to a similar DA nearby. This may be as good as you can get with some councils. But if the precedent has been set with other DAs in the areas, you have a better shot at getting yours approved.

How do I know whether to buy a 2 bedder with no carport or a 5-bedroom, 3-bath, with a double garage?

Well, start with your local expert. Your property managers are the local experts when it comes to what tenants want.

They will know if people have been looking for a 4, 2 & 2, or a studio apartment. Call up 3 or 4 property managers to get an average of what type of properties are sought-after by tenants in those suburbs.

Before we get to the fun part, let me list a few potential "No Go" aspects that you should be aware of when beginning your search. Use these combined with your buying rules.

1. Main roads or railway lines- If you can hear it or see it- you will be limiting your potential growth. Certainly, don't buy ON a main road.

2. Low-set blocks with drainage that runs towards the house. Big NO.

3. Asbestos. Anything Fibro from the 70s or earlier most likely contains asbestos, so be aware. It's not a deal killer, but you may need to factor in extra costs for removal in

the future and potentially no income while any asbestos issues are being corrected.

4. Cracks in the foundations. Obviously.

5. Zoning. Some properties are dual-zoned and may not allow a rebuild or DA because of it. Check with the local town planner.

6. Housing commissions. Three blocks over and you may be fine. Right next to, and renters may have an issue. You may miss out on great potential tenants.

   Steer clear of these and you will give your investment every chance of great capital growth.

Add those to your buying requirements.

NOW, it's time to jump onto Domain or Real estate.com.au. YES, we are there at last. Go through and shortlist 5 – 10 properties that might be acceptable in your price range.

Also, call up real estate agents and have them put your details and requirements down for an alert. Mind you, in a hot market, they won't call, though if you are lucky, you might get an email.

But in a slowing market, they may chase you up if they find a property that meets your specifications.

Once you have done your inspections and narrowed your selection to 2 – 3 properties, it's time to start thinking about the amount you will offer for each property.

In this scenario, you only want 1 property, but telling an agent you have placed offers on two other houses does give them and the vendor a sense of urgency to respond quickly. Again, in a hot market, that won't work, though it may when the market is cooler.

To make an offer, you can start with a verbal offer. Then if the agent thinks it's in the ballpark, they will ask you to put it in writing, so you would then email your offer and any clauses you may want.

Another way to put pressure on an agent is to get a copy of the contract for the property you want, sign it and drop it on the agent's desk. Tell them that the offer will expire in 4 hours and then walk out.

I heard about this strategy from a very well-known buyers' agent. It would certainly light a fire under the agent's backside to get a response from the vendor quickly.

So, you have just had your offer accepted. BOOM. Shit just got real.

Here is a brief 11-point step-by-step guide from pre-approval through to settlement.

1. Pre-approval: Once you have your pre-approval, you can begin looking for your ideal property.

2. Find a great house: Using your buying requirements, you make an offer and have it accepted.

3. Signed Contract of Sale: Sign and date your COS and send it through to your broker.

4. Your cooling-off period or finance clause starts now. Finance must be formally approved before they expire.

5. Valuation is on the money. The property will be valued by the lender to ensure you have not overpaid.

6. Formal Approval: Congratulations! Your loan has been approved.

7. Insurance: Now is the time to organise insurance for your property. Your broker can assist.

8. Loan Documents: Loan documents will be sent out to be signed and returned.

9. Settlement is booked. The settlement date is booked, and any outstanding funds are transferred to your solicitor/conveyancer or lender account.

10. SUCCESSFUL SETTLEMENT: BOOM! The house is yours. You did it. Pop the champagne!

11. Your property manager completes the tenant interview process. Tenants move in, and you begin receiving rent.

You are now a Property Investor!

Using these steps and the simple process above, you can rinse and repeat this process until your BC is maxed out, or you choose that you have accumulated enough property and move on to the next stage of your investment journey.

Investment Tip # 12 – Investing in different regions can help hedge your investment. Buying in different capital cities that have different property cycles or large regional towns that are in different sync to the major cities can mean that your entire portfolio does not hit a 'valley' all at the one time.

13

CROSS COLLATERALIZE: WHAT IS IT AND IS IT FOR ME?

Cross collateralization or cross securitization is when the bank views two of your properties as one property. You may have two, three, or even four loan splits, so many people get confused and think that their crossed collateralized properties are separated, but in fact, they are not.

When the bank views your properties as ONE, they will use the overall Loan to Value Ratio for any future applications you might require.

For example, House A is your Owner Occupier property, and it is valued at $800,000. You owe $500,000 on house A. House A, using the lessons from above, has $140,000 of usable equity at 80% LVR.

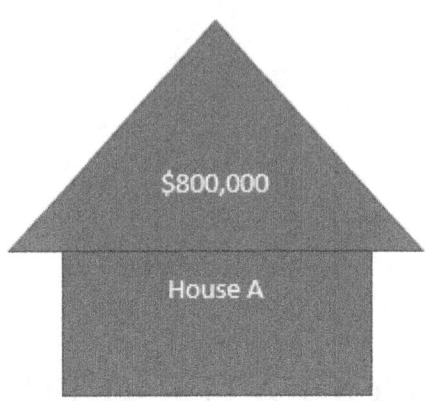

House B is one of your investment properties, and it is valued at $750,000. You still owe $600,00 on this property. House B has $0 equity at 80% LVR.

Houses A & B are cross-collateralized. They have a combined usable equity of $140,000.

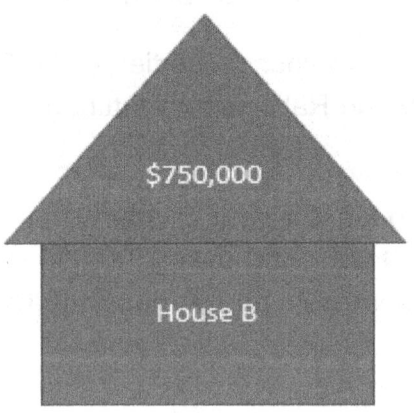

Seems fine, right? The same amount of equity as if they were separate properties. Correct. But what happens if House B goes down in value? If its value goes down to $700,000. Then you no longer have $140,000 of equity. You will only have $100,000.

See how things can start to really affect your capacity to continue buying if your properties are crossed.

Let's use another scenario where you want to sell House A and use the profits. There is $300,000 in profit there, not including real estate fees and a few other small costs.

But what if House B has now decreased even more and is only worth $550,000? If you sold, the bank would take $131,800 of your profit so that House B could be paid down to an acceptable 88% LVR, and then, LMI would be added to take the total LVR to just below 90%. Leaving you with only $168,200 profit. That's a big chunk to lose.

Or the reverse. You wanted to sell House B. To do this, you would have to increase your Owner Occupier loan on House A to $550,000 to cover the $50,000 shortfall between what you owe and the sale price (In reality, it would be more due to sales costs).

Banks love "crossing properties".

If you have gone directly to the bank to buy an investment property and own an existing property, then most likely, the bank has cross-collateralized your properties. I've seen them try to do this so many times; it should be illegal.

It creates less risk for the bank as they now have a larger asset to group together, though it creates extra risk for the investor. Speak to your broker if you are unsure if your properties might be crossed.

Let's look at another scenario that I use all the time on why crossing properties is a bad idea.

Let's say you own 5 properties—one Owner Occupied and four investment properties.

Now, picture that each property is a ship on the ocean. As they are cross-collateralized, all the anchors are linked together, representing that they are one security as viewed by the bank.

Now, picture the end ship catching fire and pulling all the other ships down with it to the bottom of the ocean. That's what crossing properties can do to your portfolio.

If you are in a negative equity situation (where your loan is higher than the value of your property) on one of your investments, or you forgot to pay the insurance that month, or your house floods, and you never had the right type of cover, the bank can sell as many of your properties as they like to regain the funds lost.

And the legal bills can be so large that they may need to sell another house to cover them. EVEN your Owner Occupier. So, unless it's an absolute emergency, don't CROSS COLLATERALIZE your properties.

When is an emergency situation, you ask?

An emergency situation might be that you have paid a large deposit ($100,000) on a property that will settle two years down the road. Two years later, you submitted your application to have your loan approved; however, the valuation has returned and it is very low.

Basically, the figures don't stack up anymore. You have no option to change lenders as your situation is very unique, and only that lender can accommodate you. You desperately don't want to lose the deposit you had already paid, and you have no buffer.

The bank requires you to pay an extra $100,000 to cover the shortfall between what they have valued the property at and what they are willing to lend you.

If you have no other means possible to beg, borrow or steal the funds, then in order to save your $100,000, it would be acceptable to cross-collateralize another property that had enough equity. However, make sure you uncross them as soon as you can.

You can uncross them by asking your broker to refinance and uncross your properties.

Investment Tip # 13 –If equity is your best friend, then cross-collateralization is your mortal enemy. Only ever cross if you are in an emergency situation.

14

OWNERSHIP STRUCTURE: OWN NAME OR A TRUST

As a caveat, please remember I am not an accountant, and nothing written here should be taken as advice. Please speak to an accountant that is great with property investment for all your taxation and ownership structure advice.

From a finance perspective, there is not too much difference between your own name and a trust, depending on the type of 'Trust.' A discretionary trust or 'Family' trust is the most common form of trust used by most investors.

These types of trusts can offer an extra level of liability protection and can be great for estate planning and succession plans within a family.

Trusts were used to evade land tax in many states as they are essentially their own entity, though, now, state governments have caught onto this practice and will trace the ownerships of trusts so that individuals can't use trusts to reduce their land tax obligation as they once did.

There is a great example of this in South Australia where the local government changed the rules regarding trusts and did not grandfather the old rules-meaning thousands of investors that had purchased properties in trusts in South Australia were suddenly hit with huge land tax bills.

Pretty unfair, in my opinion.

Something to remember with trusts is that you can't negatively gear losses in a trust. Only distribute the profits. So, if you have losses, they are kept/accrued in the trust until it begins to turn a profit.

Also, in NSW, land tax is accrued from the first dollar. So, any property you purchase in NSW under a trust will acquire land tax.

Elaborate trust structures can also be a limiting factor when looking for finance. Having trusts that have other trusts as beneficiaries or shareholders does confuse a lot of lenders, and they normally won't want to lend to these types of entities.

As my accountant says, 'If you are not likely to be litigated against, then buying in your own name is totally ok' though, again, please speak to your accountant as everybody's situation is different.

An example of how you can still minimise land tax is, if you purchase two properties in NSW, two in VIC, and two in QLD, depending on the value of the land, you will most likely dodge most land tax thresholds.

Understanding property taxation is extremely important. My current accountant saved me $20,000 in capital gains tax due to his knowledge of the PPOR rules (Primary Place Of Residence 6 year rule).

One thing to be aware of when buying in your own name is that in some states if a couple were to purchase a property with a land value of $500,000 and the property was purchased in both their names, then the $500,000 land value goes against both individuals. It's not split evenly.

This can play against you down the road, so ensuring you have your ownership structure set to benefit your current and future plans is crucial.

Investment Tip # 14 –When it comes to property tax, don't listen to your mate down the pub or a broker. Speak to an accountant knowledgeable in property investment ownership structure and property investment deductions. If you don't know a good property accountant, then give us a call and we can point you in the right direction.

15

TAX AND YOUR INVESTMENT PROPERTY

As with the previous chapter, please refer to your accountant for advice regarding tax deductions you can claim from your investment property.

As a fellow investor, I will give you, my *experience.*

Any interest paid on an investment loan, that means interest on a loan taken out to be used for investment purposes, can be claimed as a tax deduction if the corresponding asset is being rented or available for rent.

So, that includes your equity as well. If it was released and used for investment purposes, then it can be claimed as a deduction. Plus, lending costs (except stamp duty), bank fees, and discharge fees can all be claimed.

Depreciation Schedule:

Getting a depreciation schedule is a must for every investor, as this can add a lot of extra cash flow to your investment at tax time.

Though, there is a caveat with any depreciation schedule. Yes, it may seem like free money (and I've seen a very entertaining quantity surveyor use the catchline 'FREE MONEY' repeatedly), particularly if your property is new and you are claiming back over $10,000 a year in the first few years, HOWEVER, if you sell your property all the deductions you claimed through depreciation will cause your cost basis to be adjusted by the ATO.

This may slightly increase the Capital Gains tax you have to pay.

But if you have a strategy of NEVER selling any of your properties, then you may end up being compensated for that depreciating asset while never having to pay back that money. FREE MONEY—Maybe. It's definitely food for thought.

There are all sorts of specific rules regarding repairs versus replacement, so ensure you know the difference. Your property management fees, insurance, energy bills, water, and council rates are all tax-deductible.

Just remember that your property must be available for rent for you to claim the interest as a deduction. So, advertising it as soon as you receive the keys is vital, even if you take a few weeks or two months to choose a tenant, (you may need to complete a small renovation), if you see what I mean.

Please remember that you should speak to an accountant with a solid understanding of property investment to help you decide what ownership structure to use when purchasing your investment properties.

Investment Tip # 15 –All together now!! If you never sell your investments, depreciation is Free Money!!

16

HOW TO PROTECT YOUR INVESTMENT

With such a large amount of money on the line, it can be very scary to think about losing it all if something goes wrong.

From fires to floods to tenant damage, there are a hundred things that could happen to your investment. And there are only three ways to protect yourself from that 1-in-100 year event.

1. Due Diligence prior to purchasing,

2. Insurance,

3. Great tenant selection.

With Due Diligence, you can ensure you are not in a flood zone or that your property is situated high enough that it will never be affected by flooding. Same for bushfires. It is also applicable to suburbs that may be more prone to break-ins and robberies. These are all events that can be mostly mitigated by buying in the right area.

With Insurance events such as accidental tenant damage right through to the neighbour's car crashing into your living room, can all have the risk removed through insurance.

Landlords' Insurance, and House and Contents Insurance (if you have particular items you have left in the property) can ensure that when the proverbial does hit the fan, you can be confident you will be repaid for the cost of your investment.

So, please update your insurance every year as your property increases in value and add a little bit extra to cover the demolition and removal of your existing property. That alone can leave you $50,000 short if that 1-in-100 event ever came to pass.

And remember that your personal insurances are just as important- if you break your leg and can't work for six months, will you be able to still cover your mortgage repayments?

Great tenant selection includes selecting a great property manager that will collect rent on time, will select great tenants, and will ensure your investment is looked after.

Investment Tip # 16 –Insurance is required by every lender when you buy, and without it, you open yourself up to major risk. Just pay for it. It's a deduction. It's one of those necessary evils.

17

WAYS TO CREATE CAPITAL GROWTH IN YOUR PROPERTY

There are three main ways for your property to grow in value.

They are:

Let the market do its thing:

The main set-and-forget way to create growth is to do nothing.

That is, let the market do its thing, and inevitably, if you have purchased in a sought-after area with good access to schools, hospitals, and transportation, in a population greater than 50,000 people with a growing populous, in a suburb with a rental market of around 30% and a vacancy rate of below 2.5%, with a historical capital growth rate of 5-10%- then your property will increase in value.

No questions asked. It's only a matter of time.

Over the past 80 years, Australian property markets have followed a natural valleys and peaks cycle of increased growth. With there being close to a one million home shortage in

Australia at this moment in time, supply issues only getting worse, and 250-300,000 people migrating to Australia every year, there is not a plausible/realistic scenario where average prices for all of Australia fall by more than 20%

In the last 80 years, the most property prices have fallen prior to the current low is between 5-7% depending on which figures you use. And the current market correction (after seeing a 20-32% increase in 12 months) might still only turn out to be 10% in total, across all major capitals, once the dust settles.

As with any unsustainable growth cycle there is a correction. It's simple economics and should be expected to occur occasionally.

Don't get me wrong- there will be people that overextend themselves and have to sell, though the majority of people will be able to tighten their belts and ride out the current wave of rate rises.

One important measure to remember when trying to assess how much prices will go down is the price of a new build. If the cost to build a new property at today's market prices has not gone down (which it has not), then that creates a line in the sand for all other future properties.

SO, the increases in construction costs have, in one way, placed a floor under the Australian property market. Unless construction materials and labour costs decrease by a great margin then these entry-level properties cannot drop further.

It's also why higher-value properties can have much larger variations and swings when there is a downturn.

For example- a $25 million dollar property's value is based on land value and a lot of very expensive fixtures and fittings. The value of these three things is very subjective when no longer new. And these can devalue greatly during a market low.

However, a standard $650,000 new build would probably only drop by around $50,000.

I have seen over a thousand bank valuations in the last decade and even in this so-called "biggest market correction in history," prices are not being valued down by more than $50,000 on a standard $650,000 build.

Food for thought…

So let the market do its thing, and your property will double, triple or even quadruple if given enough time.

For example, in 2002, I purchased a property for $169,000. We sold it in 2018 for $517,000. So, our property tripled in value (and we sold at the bottom of the market. It was valued at $80,000 more just six months prior) in 16 years.

That means every 5.3 years it increased in value by the amount we originally purchased it for.

The property was purchased in a lower socio-economic suburb that bordered two other much better suburbs.

Gentrification took place as it does, and within 5 years, it had become one of the edgy places for young families to live. The market did its thing.

Create Growth:

Another way to create growth is to improve the asset that resides on the land. Yes, the value is in the land, but that will remain relatively stable for a long time.

The depreciating asset that sits on that land can be improved and made fresh. From a complete overhaul renovation or a cosmetic touch-up, properties can have tens of thousands or millions of dollars added to their value in this way. For those that are pretty handy or have a trade, you can literally make a living by buying and renovating properties to flip or hold.

As a guide for cosmetic renovations, if you want the best bang for your buck, a new paint job on the exterior and interior, some easy fresh landscaping, removing any vegetation that covers the profile of the property and doing a new kitchen and bathroom on the cheap- using a Bunnings' kitchen pack- will add $100,000 or more to a property's valuation.

We carried out a cosmetic renovation on an investment property. It cost us $36,000 to replace the kitchen and the bathroom (except for the bath), paint all internal and external walls, install a fence, add ceiling fans, add a wardrobe, and have a barn door slider fitted. When the property was revalued, we added $120,000.

A 3 to 1 ratio of expenses to value should be your goal too.

Add another dwelling or subdivide:

The third way is to subdivide, add a granny flat or strata title your property. If you own a duplex, then strata titling which creates individual titles for your two properties means they will be valued separately, can drastically increase the value of both properties.

Adding a granny flat can add instant cash flow (that will be accepted as income by the bank, unlike renting a room out in your own home). It can also add value to any resale as it is essentially two homes on one title now.

Subdividing is another great way to make full use of your property's extra land. Many places have 300-400 sqm of side and rear space that is basically just grassed backyards.

Under the right conditions, this can be subdivided to create another lot and can be sold or constructed to supercharge your growth.

Investment Tip # 17 – If you have a trade or have tradie friends, now is a good time to start buttering them up. They can help add tens of thousands to the value of your property.

18

HOW MANY PROPERTIES DO I NEED?

So, that question is a little bit rigged. Sorry. The number of properties you will need in your portfolio will depend on your family structure and your end goals.

If you have a family of 5 and need to build an income source for you, your partner and three kids, and to create generational wealth then you will need more properties than a single individual with no children who only wants an income of $120,000 a year.

Let's run a few different scenarios, so you can get an idea of the growth potential and the number of properties required.

Hint: It's not as many as you think.

For a family of 5 wanting to retire on an income of $150,000:

Let's game this out.

Scenario: Couple A already have an Owner-Occupied property that they have owned for many years, before deciding they want to invest. In this, and every scenario, the earlier you begin purchasing property the better. But it's not a requirement, so don't be discouraged.

For all scenarios, we have used an interest rate of 4.5% P+I Variable for the Owner Occupied and 5.5% P+I Variable for any investment properties. The average of where rates will be when they hopefully begin to come back down in 6-12 months.

2024 Stage 3 tax rates have been assumed, though they will only differ from current tax rates by around $10,000 if they are not enacted by the current government.

Remember our A, B, & C.

Couple A, refinance (A), release enough equity for 2 deposits (B) and obtain a pre-approval (C). They purchase a $600,000 investment property for which they receive roughly $500 a week in rent.

6 months later, Couple A purchases another $600,000 investment property receiving the same amount of rent.

Couple A now spends two years budgeting well and paying extra into their Owner-Occupied Home loan. In the 3rd year, Couple A releases equity from their two investment properties and purchases two more investment properties of similar values and similar rental returns as their previous investment properties.

Click on the below link to run the "Extra Repayments Calculator." Extra Repayment Calculator or head to www.opfinance.com.au/calculators

The couple continues to pay any extra funds into their Oocc loan through their offset account or redraw (as their own home loan is not tax-deductible). At year 5, they release one last amount of equity from whichever property has accumulated enough equity and purchase one more property for a similar price and receive similar rent.

The below scenario is a 15-year time frame, with a few specific adjustments that will allow you to reach your goal in the time frame required. I have used very conservative growth rates that are far below the national average for most states and suburbs in Australia.

At the end of their accumulation (purchasing) and consolidation (finished buying and let growth occur) stages, their portfolio will look like this.

Scenario 1:

Year Purchased	Purchase Price	Price Est in 2038	Loan when Purchased	Loan Amount in 2038
O-Occ 2012	$600,000	$2,000,000	$528,000	0
2023 Inv1	$600,000	$1,200,000	$600,000	$333,000
2023 Inv2	$600,000	$1,200,000	$600,000	$333,000
2026 Inv3	$600,000	$1,200,000	$600,000	$382,000

2026 Inv4	$600,000	$1,200,000	$600,000	$382,000
2028 Inv5	$600,000	$1,000,000	$600,000	$427,000
Total	$3,600,000	$7,800,000	$3,600,000	$1,857,000

By paying an extra $1,500 into your Owner Occupier loan until paid down and an extra $300 into your investment properties each month, the 15-year time frame can be achieved and will most likely be beaten.

 Yes we are breaking the "pay down your home loan before any tax deductible debt" but in this case they are working in conjunction and the NO DEBT goal will be achieved sooner due to the compounding of paying extra.

This is an extra $36,000 a year from when you purchase your last property. It seems like a lot though, let's finish the scenario and then work backwards.

At the end of our consolidation phase, we sell two properties worth $2,200,000 and pay off all debt. This would leave around $340,000 in profit, though after capital gains tax and their respective tax burdens they will be left with:

Couple A would be left with a fully paid-off Owner Occupier property worth $2,000,000 and a $3,600,000 investment portfolio completely debt-free.

Please use the link below to play and run your own scenarios and what they might look like. Extra Repayment Calculator or head to www.opfinance.com.au/calculators

Rental income on a $3,600,000 portfolio at a 4.5% Yield would be around $162,000 a year, not counting property management fees. Property management fees might be around 7% which would leave us with $150,660 a year in income.

OR with advice from a good financial planner, you could sell your properties and purchase high-yield dividend stocks earning 6%. Your return would then be $216,000 a year.

In summary: You will be debt-free and have an income of about $160,000 – $215,000 a year, depending on how you transition your portfolio. All done in 15 years. The compounding interest effect of paying more into your home loans means for an extra $3,000 a month, you can be retired in 15 years earning more money each year than you could probably ever spend.

The options, once you have built and paid down a portion of your portfolio, are endless, and I recommend speaking to a financial planner/advisor to get advice on how to distribute your gains. The point here is to see that property is the number one tool in Australia to create that initial wealth.

After your portfolio is built, well, you may be tired of dealing with tenants and decide to put your wealth elsewhere. Having the problem of where to put your millions is a great problem to have.

I'll get to the question, "What if you don't pay any extra into your portfolio shortly."

Now, let's say you only paid an extra $1500 on your Owner Occupier loan each month and nothing extra on your investments, and you wanted to retire in 10 years, not 15. Let's look at the figures.

Scenario 2:

Year Purchased	Purchase Price	Price Est in 2033	Loan when Purchased	Loan Amount in 2033
O-Occ 2012	$600,000	$1,700,000	$528,000	$0
2023 Inv1	$600,000	$1,000,000	$600,000	$488,000
2023 Inv2	$600,000	$1,000,000	$600,000	$488,000
2026 Inv3	$600,000	$1,000,000	$600,000	$527,000
2026 Inv4	$600,000	$1,000,000	$600,000	$527,000
2028 Inv5	$600,000	$950,000	$600,000	$550,000
Total	$3,600,000	$6,650,000	$3,600,000	$2,580,000

Using very conservative estimates where your properties have only increased by less than 80% after 10 years, the figures now show a total portfolio value of $6,650,000 and debt of $2,580,000.

If we use the same strategy of selling properties to pay off debt, we will have the following.

We sell three properties worth $2,950,000 and pay off all debt. This would leave around $370,000, though after CGT and their own tax burden they would have:

Couple A would be left with a fully paid-off Owner Occupied property worth $1,700,000, and a $2,000,000 portfolio completely paid off.

Rental income on a $2,000,000 portfolio would be around $99,000 a year, not counting property management fees.

Or you could sell your properties and go with the high-yield dividend option again. Your return would be $120,000 a year for the rest of your life. Not bad for 10 years of investing.

Now, if you were to not pay any extra off your Owner Occupied loan over 10 years and you just paid the bare minimum, the results would be as follows.

Scenario 3:

Year Purchased	Purchase Price	Price Est in 2033	Loan when Purchased	Loan Amount in 2033
O-Occ 2012	$600,000	$1,700,000	$528,000	$255,000
2023 Inv1	$600,000	$1,000,000	$600,000	$481,000
2023 Inv2	$600,000	$1,000,000	$600,000	$481,000
2026 Inv3	$600,000	$1,000,000	$600,000	$532,000
2026 Inv4	$600,000	$1,000,000	$600,000	$532,000
2028 Inv5	$600,000	$950,000	$600,000	$544,000
Total	$3,600,000	$6,650,000	$3,600,000	$2,825,000

Using the same very conservative estimates where your properties have only increased by less than 80% after 10 years, the figures now show a total portfolio value of $6,650,000 and debt of $2,825,000.

If we use the same strategy of selling properties to pay off debt, we will have the following:

After CGT and your tax burden you will still be $80,000 short after the sale of your properties. ☹

Well, you still own $1,950,000 worth of investment property that you are collecting 100% of the rent on. In 9 months, you will have received enough rent to pay your tax bill, and then, you are home-free with a portfolio of almost 2 million dollars and a fully paid down Owner Occupier.

Again, if you were to sell the remaining properties and go with the high-yield dividend option, your return would be $117,000 a year. Not bad for 10 years of investing and not paying a cent more than you had to into your loan.

What would a 15-year time frame and not paying any extra look like?

Scenario 4:

Year Purchased	Purchase Price	Price Est in 2038	Loan when Purchased	Loan Amount in 2038
O-Occ 2012	$600,000	$2,000,000	$528,000	$137,000
2023 Inv1	$600,000	$1,200,000	$600,000	$407,000
2023 Inv2	$600,000	$1,200,000	$600,000	$407,000
2026 Inv3	$600,000	$1,200,000	$600,000	$458,000
2026 Inv4	$600,000	$1,200,000	$600,000	$458,000
2028 Inv5	$600,000	$1,000,000	$600,000	$488,000
Total	$3,600,000	$7,800,000	$3,600,000	$2,355,000

Couple A would be left with a fully paid-off Owner Occupied property worth $2,000,000 and a $2,645,000 portfolio completely paid off.

Rental income on a $2,645,000 portfolio would be around $119,025 a year, not counting property management fees or $110,693 after paying a 7% management fee.

Or sell your properties and go with the high-yield dividend option again. Your return would be $158,700 a year.

But what if you **never sold** and only made the bare minimum repayments?

Scenario 5:

Year Purchased	Purchase Price	Price Est in 2058	Loan when Purchased	Loan Amount at in 2058
O-Occ 2012	$600,000	$4,000,000	$528,000	0
2023 Inv1	$600,000	$2,200,000	$600,000	$0
2023 Inv2	$600,000	$2,200,000	$600,000	$0
2026 Inv3	$600,000	$2,200,000	$600,000	$0
2026 Inv4	$600,000	$2,200,000	$600,000	$0
2028 Inv5	$600,000	$2,000,000	$600,000	$0
Total	$3,600,000	$14,800,000	$3,600,000	$0

In this example as you have paid your Owner Occupier debt completely by 2042 you continued to pay the remaining properties off over their full 30-year terms. You would still own all properties, have no debt and have a portfolio worth (very large factor of error here as it's so far into the future) around $14,800,000. I do think this is still being very conservative considering the time frame. Rent on a portfolio of that size would be over $400,000 a year after property management fees. So, if you are prepared to play the long game your returns can be astronomical.

The examples above are all broad descriptions of how you can use just a handful of properties to build wealth in a relatively short period and then use that wealth to fund your retirement or whatever your goal might be.

If you think of property as the vehicle or the tool that you will use to start your wealth creation journey, then you will be on the right path.

As mentioned, the examples above are extremely conservative. Imagine if your properties doubled in 6 or 7 years? What sort of income could they return then?

What if "I'm single?" you may ask. Well, then the task is harder as your borrowing capacity will be lower, BUT the other side of the coin is that you don't need 5 or 6 properties. You can actually make do with just 3 or 4.

So, when you see people sprouting about having a ten-property portfolio or see books titled, 'How I built a 300-property portfolio,' you can just say to yourself, 'Well, I only need 6.'

By choosing a strategy you decide fits your goals and risk profile and then research that strategy until you feel you can implement it, you are taking control of your personal situation Or if you decide that it's potentially too complicated for you to handle by yourself, find an expert that uses that strategy and hire their expertise to fulfil your goals. You now have all the pieces, all the tips and tricks and see how they all fit together. You can now choose how your financial future plays out.

If this all seems too complicated then don't fret. We do these exact scenarios every day of the week, the Open Plan Finance team are here to educate and talk you through every step of the way, if that's what you require.

Investment Tip # 18 – If you strategize right, you can build your entire portfolio in a very short time. 12-18 months of planning can cut down your acquisition phase by five or more years.

19

PUT YOUR FEET UP -YOU HAVE EARNED IT

After delving into the intricacies of how to build and then completely pay down a multimillion-dollar property portfolio, you deserve a wine or a beer.

I would like you to put your feet up while reading this last chapter. You now know more than 99% of property owners in Australia.

You now have the knowledge of how to map your course to retirement (if that's your goal). Out of all the asset classes, I truly believe that property is the best way to create wealth, potentially, generational wealth.

If it takes you 10 or fifteen years to achieve a goal, you're probably not going to squander the gains because you worked damn hard for them. You will savour them. You will recognise the sweet struggle and see that it was worth it.

You now know that budgeting is just as important in the beginning as your income is. When your income increases and your debt level decreases, your borrowing capacity increases. That you should only pay a deposit once and once only, and that equity really is your golden ticket. It is The Equity Advantage so make the most of it.

You have learned that Due Diligence will stop you from buying a crappy investment. How to create a strategy and to re-assess which strategy to use after each purchase.

You now understand that without finance, none of this is possible. And that you should, in 99% of cases, never cross-collateralize your properties.

You saw that ownership structure is key and should be thought of early and with an eye to the future.

You can see how tax affects your portfolio, how to protect your assets and finally, how many properties you need in order to retire and on what sort of income.

Remember that if the best time to buy property was 20 years ago, then the 2nd best time to buy a property is today!

You only need 6 properties. You have 6 blocks to place. That's all. Only 6. Some of you may be onto your second or third already. You only have to get to 6.

Now, go out there and use the Equity Advantage and place your 6 blocks.

By Jason Hare

Property Investor, Finance Consultant & Founder of Open Plan Finance

https://www.opfinance.com.au/

https://www.facebook.com/groups/13354200728300

https://www.linkedin.com/in/jason-hare-32348a154/

jason@opfinance.com.au

Property Investor Flow Chart

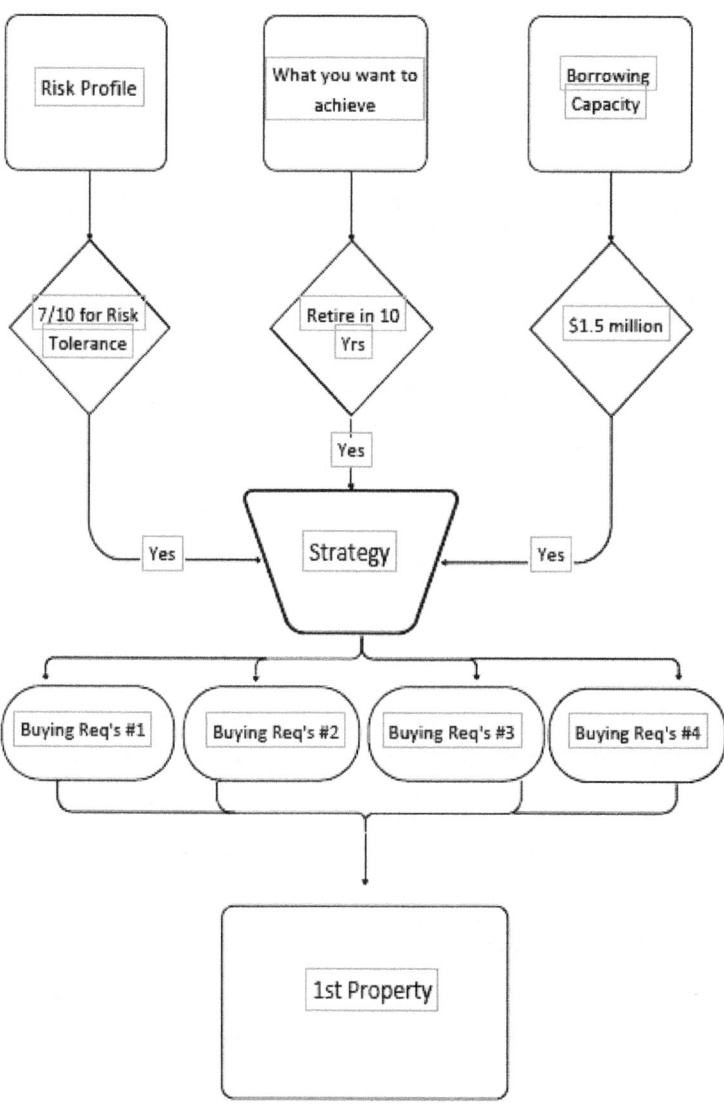

Risk Profile

What you want to achieve

Borrowing Capacity

7/10 for Risk Tolerance

Retire in 10 Yrs

$1.5 million

Yes

Yes

Strategy

Yes

Buying Req's #1

Buying Req's #2

Buying Req's #3

Buying Req's #4

1st Property

Made in the USA
Monee, IL
07 July 2026

56552024R00079